CULTURE SHOCK!
Britain

Terry Tan

Graphic Arts Center Publishing Company
Portland, Oregon

In the same series

Australia	Italy	South Africa
Borneo	Japan	Spain
Burma	Korea	Sri Lanka
Canada	Malaysia	Syria
China	Morocco	Taiwan
France	Nepal	Thailand
Hong Kong	Norway	USA
India	Pakistan	Vietnam
Indonesia	Philippines	
Israel	Singapore	

Illustrations by TRIGG
Photographs by Terry Tan
Cover photographs by Bira de Silveira

© 1992 Times Editions Pte Ltd
Reprinted 1994, 1995

This book is published by special
arrangement with Times Editions Pte Ltd
Times Centre, 1 New Industrial Road, Singapore 1953
International Standard Book Number 1-55868-061-6
Library of Congress Catalog Number 91-72723
Graphic Arts Center Publishing Company
P.O. Box 10306 • Portland, Oregon 97210 • (503) 226-2402

Printed in Singapore

CONTENTS

INTRODUCTION

It was in 1968 that I first set foot on British soil, on one of those charter packages that cost a fraction of what they would today but at considerable cost to plane comfort. I think I was enamoured of the place. Since the age of six, my friends and I had been bombarded with the history of the British Empire and the Commonwealth, Keats, Wordsworth and Shakespeare. And it didn't end in the school. At Monopoly, I was buying and selling Park Lane and Mayfair properties long before I strolled along these avenues. My history, geography and literature teachers were Welsh, Scottish and Irish, and they brought to life what I learnt from books. The daily morning assemblies were raised voices in homage of the *Men of Harlech*. In this way Anglophilia rubbed off many of us.

When I actually set foot on British soil, it was with a feeling of curious excitement about seeing first hand the land I had read so much about. Or Monopoly come home. Primarily, it has been an extended sojourn: geography, literature and history come to life and an education process no less absorbing than one about any culture outside one's own. That four-week holiday merely skimmed the surface of 'touristy' Britain, but it was enough to intrigue me about the whole British psyche. National pride aside, I have always subscribed to an open mind about life beyond my doorstep. The reasons why I have chosen to live and work in Britain since 1983 were as much providence as a logical result of being immersed in British mores for the better part of my school life.

Having made the decision to come here, it would have been blinkered and negative not to assimilate, observe, learn and generally be at ease within an alien environment. Despite my early years of being steeped in Anglophilia, Britain was, and still is, essentially alien. You can at best come to grips with the problems and co-exist with them, but never become British, whatever your residential status. Only with the confidence that nothing can take away your cultural heritage can you be comfortable in a foreign land. The old adage 'Any place you hang your hat is home' applies only when you've got your head screwed on right. Like not harbouring feelings of inadequacy, inferiority and all the other -ities that cloud your sense of identity and belonging, wherever your hatstand. In the eight years that I have actually thrust myself into the mainstream of British life, it has been a process rife with problems, complications, crosswires, joy and satisfaction. I had to rid myself of preconceived notions, prejudices and hang-ups to make the best of my decision. I choose deliberately to mix with the British, cultivate their friendship and build up my store of life's knowledge. I did not want to end up as a statistic in reports about social integration problems among émigrés. This remains so with many foreigners who came to live in Britain by their own volition or for political reasons.

It is impossible to give a blanket statement about life in an adopted country because of the variables. In my long observations of the British, I have encountered many things that are at odds with my own philosophy but as much that I have embraced with enthusiasm. Their sense of fair play, integrity, humour, the sublime and the ridiculous. Fundamentally, it's the realisation that I am different from them rather than the other way round. I am the foreigner and most of the accommodation has to come from my quarter. The British are no different from any other race in basic terms – they just talk, live and pursue their ambitions in different ways. You either muddle through or glide with them.

I have had my nose to the British ground, my ears to British sounds and my eyes on British idiosyncrasies with the objective of understanding – not changing – them. The best I hope to offer in return for getting under their skin is to let them under mine. In this light, I am better able to understand why British colonialists were the way they were, never giving up a slice of their Britishness even in the depths of a Malayan rubber plantation. It is likewise for many immigrants here. Richer are those who assimilate without clouding their sense of identity.

I have learnt to be patient the British way and not get flustered because service people don't jump when I call. I have had to handle household chores with dignity and stop moaning about the dearth of cheap labour. Most important, I have to think British to survive. It's got nothing to do with the loss of identity and everything to do with doing as the Romans do. The difference between uncomfortable existence and total peace of mind. I hope *Culture Shock! Britain* will ease you into the country. If I have had to generalise in many instances, it's because there is no way to be specific; regard the information as a springboard towards your own astute analyses. While I have done a fair amount of research, much else is the result of personal experience gleaned from constant exposure.

Chapter One

BRITANNIA

When you consider that most Australians and North Americans trace back their ancestry to the British Isles, it is not surprising that thousands of them come seeking their roots every year. The more prosaic come to find work or simply to assuage the inexplicable Anglophile need. But by contrast to its former colonies, the British Isles is a mere minnow to their whale. Some 60 million people are crammed into what is not altogether rolling downs and dappled woodlands. Britain's inner cities can be a grim picture of urban rot, decay, overcrowding and mean streets.

Many British children have never seen a cow or even a live chicken, having been born and brought up in urban concrete sprawls.

Travel is relatively expensive, and many poor families would not think of spending their cash on such things.

The tourist brochures naturally sidestep the existence of these depressing urban pockets. Which visitor would find anything remotely romantic about a tenement block with scrubby, graffiti-laden walls, gloomy stairwells and sinister nooks? However, it is a blight that the present government, with the backing of Prince Charles, is working very hard at alleviating.

Vehicular traffic and all that goes with it – pollution, lead contamination and plain hassle – are a part of Britain's transportation network which is constantly subject to environmentalist review. The green policy, fear of the hole in the ozone layer getting larger, acid rain, etc., are all issues very much under the skin and conscience of the enlightened British. Of course there are millions whose concern ends at their doorstep and who do not care about what is happening to society.

As a newly arrived visitor (whether for a short stay or long term), the option of whether to get involved with green issues or not is yours. But you will be hard put to ignore public outcry about the destruction of the earth, the disappearance of rain forests thousands of miles away, ivory poaching and the hundred and one causes that prickle the conscience of millions of British. This is a country that has a markedly contrasting mix of humanity – those totally indifferent and insular and those passionately concerned about what is happening to the world.

In a capsule, if it is at all possible, the British Isles can offer you a completely fulfilling life, a choice of pastoral idyll or city razzmatazz; you can be quirky or sombrely serious, outrageous or plain lascivious. You 'pays your money and you takes your choice', and almost everyone minds his own business, usually looking away when someone else is indulging in weird behaviour. But first a brief description of the country and a few statistics to ease you into what hopefully will be a stay of endless delights.

BRITAIN AT A GLANCE

From north to south, Britain can be divided into the following regions: the Scottish Highlands, the Scottish Lowlands, the North, Wales, the Midlands, East Anglia, the West Country and the Southeast. Each region is composed of several counties with major cities and towns which are in turn divided into boroughs and dotted liberally with villages. For instance, in London, Kensington, Camden, Chelsea, etc. are boroughs. The descriptions below do not refer to specific counties but rather point to a loose amalgam of areas and regions with similar geographical characteristics often reflected in their popular names, for example the Lake District or the Cotswolds, which may embrace counties as a whole or in part.

The Thames Valley

A historic link from London to Oxfordshire, the Thames Valley embraces the royal county of Berkshire where stands Windsor Castle, the capital of London and its environs, Eton, Henley of the regatta and Sonning, regarded as the prettiest Tudor village of all.

Oxford is not only an ancient university town, but a name given to many things from shoes to trousers. Not far is Blenheim Palace, birthplace of former prime minister Winston Churchill.

The Cotswolds

The Thames River takes its source in this region, in the village of Bell Weir Lock. This waterway gushes from a region known for its weathered honey-coloured stone used for building. The Cotswolds is rich with history from ancient Roman ruins in Cirencester to Shakespeare's birthplace in Stratford-upon-Avon. Once the wool centre, it is the foundation of much of Britain's post industrial wealth. From here, England's major waterway is a delightful cruise through history, hundreds of quaint villages, pastoral sights and handsome towns. Some of Britains's most idyllic villages are nestled within its bosom, like the picture-postcard Bourton-on-the-Water.

Wessex

To the south of London, Wessex is more a historical than a geographical description of Thomas Hardy country and other literary luminaries, once an ancient kingdom of the West Saxons that embraced what are now the counties of Berkshire, Hampshire, Wiltshire, Dorset and Somerset. From Winchester Cathedral's magnificence to the mystique of Stonehenge at Salisbury Plain, history permeates the whole region. The Victorian coastal watering hole of Bournemouth is still a popular resort to 'take the air'.

Kent & Sussex

These geological twin counties lie at England's most southeastern tip. Blessed by Mother Nature, the region is a splendiferous orchard where one of the greatest joys of summer is to pick your own fruit.

Even on a cold blustery day, Brighton Pier has a holiday feeling with its candy floss and toffee apples stall.

13

Eat as much as you like, free under the apple, pear, cherry or plum tree and pay for what you can cart away. The coast is very popular with holiday makers, dotted as it is with the seaside resorts of Brighton, Eastbourne, Dover, Sandwich, Ramsgate and Margate.

East Anglia

A region of gentility and aristocratic heritage, East Anglia comprises Suffolk, Norfolk, Cambridgeshire and Essex in the rather isolated 'hump' of Southeast England to the north of London. This is a region of rolling downs, gentle hills, lush valleys and floral excess. The British royal family's private home of Sandringham is in Norfolk with 6916 acres (2800 hectares) of parkland open to the public. The university town of Cambridge was founded by a group of Franciscans, Dominicans and Benedictines. The first college was founded by Oxford scholars who had fled their town after a disagreement with the authorities in 1209.

The Norfolk Broads are excellent for barge and boating holidays, being largely inaccessible to cars.

Suffolk is Constable country. The artist's paintings of Suffolk landscapes are today a priceless part of the English heritage.

The West Country

This area embraces Dorset, Somerset, Devon and Cornwall at England's westernmost tip and the aptly named village of Land's End. England's maritime heritage is enshrined here, an area of romance and dark history. Exmoor and Dartmoor are national parks with moorland evocative of mystery and evil deeds. Bodmin Moor in Cornwall is the setting for Daphne Du Maurier's *Jamaica Inn* which still stands as a delightful pub full of the writer's memorabilia. Penzance and Plymouth exude the spirit of discovery and exploration from where Francis Drake, Walter Raleigh and the Pilgrim Fathers set out in search of adventure.

The Lake District

Britain's most visited area, the Lake District possesses the most stunning scenery within the smallest area: no more than 31 by 18.5 miles (50 kilometres by 30 kilometres). Nestled among gentle hills and dappled woodlands, sparkling lakes and shimmering tarns mirror the magnificence of more rugged and misty peaks. The Lake District includes the western half of Cumbria and is distinct for its beauty and charm.

Birthplace of William Wordsworth and Beatrix Potter, the Lake District is now increasingly congested with millions of tourists coming to soak up the poetic ambience. Kendal, Ambleside, Grasmere, Windermere and Keswick are picture-postcard places – once you find a parking place.

Much of the British countryside is a scene of pastoral tranquility such as the one shown in this picture.

The North

Immediately south of Scotland, the north of England embraces the counties of Northumbria, County Durham, Humberside and Lancashire, and the three ridings of Yorkshire. Here industrial depression is cheek by jowl with stunning and wild scenic beauty, from the Yorkshire Moors and Dales down to the Peak District. Major cities include Newcastle-upon-Tyne on the northeast coast, and Manchester, Sheffield and Leeds skirting the Peak District National Park. The Pennines, England's backbone of hills, are topped by the long distance footpath of the Pennine Way, a formidable challenge to walkers stretching 248 miles (400 kilometres) from the Peak through Yorkshire and Northumbria, finishing on the border of Scotland. The Roman emperor Hadrian built his fortified wall of 72.5 miles (117 kilometres) from sea to sea to keep out the marauding Scots in AD 120. Yorkshire is reminiscent of the Brontë literary family. The delightful medieval city of York houses York Minster, the largest Gothic cathedral in England.

Scotland

With its untamed landscapes, Scotland offers a mind-boggling number of ancient edifices to be explored, including some 4000 castles. Not a part of England, it is a separate country with a separate and distinct sense of pride and identity. Scotland is divided into Highlands and Lowlands, also described as Southern Uplands. Historic sites are Edinburgh Castle dominating the country's capital, which is surprisingly small but elegant; Linlithgow, the birthplace of Mary Queen of Scots; and St Andrews in the Kingdom of Fife, the birthplace of golf.

Across the estuary of the Firth of Forth are the Highlands and the towering crags of the Grampian Mountains. Most of the settlement is along the coast. Major cities are Elgin, Inverness and Dundee with the major tourist attraction being Loch Ness. The monster's existence is still a hotly debated point.

Wales

With its impossibly complex language – the oldest in Europe – and lusty voices, Wales has a rustic charm all its own. While South Wales is mostly industrial, North Wales is a country of exceptional beauty and rugged charm, especially Snowdonia that rivals the Lake District for scenic beauty. The Welsh are fiercely proud of their ancient heritage, unshaken in their belief that they are the true Britons. Due west of the Midlands, Wales lies beyond the Severn Bridge if you come along the M4 or A40 from London. The sign that reads 'Croeso i Cymru' means 'Welcome to Wales'. Cymru is the Welsh name for the country.

The Channel Islands

Guernsey, Jersey, Alderney and Sark are an autonomous democracy in their own right with their own currency; Great Britain only looks after their foreign policy and defence. Little pockets of Gallic charm reflecting their historical links with France, the islands are less than an hour away by air. Only 7.5 miles (12 kilometres) from the French coast, these islands are tax havens for the rich.

The Isle of Man

Like the Channel Islands, the Isle of Man has its own parliament, tax laws, currency and stamps. It is also a tax haven for the rich who don't like to pay British taxes. Lying in the Irish Sea midway between Northern Ireland and the Lake District's coast, the island is most notable for its Grand Prix circuit and the tailless Manx cat.

STATISTICS

England

Area: 52,000 square miles (130,000 square kilometres)
Population: 47 million
Political status: Constitutional monarchy

Capital: London, with 6.7 million residents swelled daily to around 10 million by commuters, day-trippers and tourists.
Language: English
Currency: £ sterling, 100p to the pound; £1 pieces, 50p, 20p, 10p, 5p, 2p and 1p. Scottish currency is also accepted.

Scotland

Area: 31,200 square miles (78,000 square kilometres)
Population: 5.2 million
Political status: Constitutional monarchy
Capital: Edinburgh, with 435,000 residents
Language: English with some Gaelic spoken in the Western Isles
Currency: Scottish £. English and Scottish bank notes are interchangeable

Wales

Area: 832 square miles (2080 square kilometres)
Population: 2.7 million
Political status: Principality of Great Britain
Capital: Cardiff, with 260,000 inhabitants
Language: 80% English, 20% Welsh
Currency: same as England

LONDON

London lays bare the soul of the most stoic; one might be shocked, reviled, seduced or mesmerised, but few people remain unmoved by this beguiling city. It is totally pardonable to see London as a microcosm of England – Britain even – for its phantasmagorical offering of life, although people who live outside London would strongly disagree. It does, after all, have a little (or a lot) of everything that is good, bad, excessive, tasteful, shocking and pleasing. I have rarely heard less ambivalent feelings about this sprawling city that

London is a fascinating blend of old and new, ugly and beautiful, refinement and coarseness; in fact, it is the very essence of life.

provokes extremes in sentiment. Leaving this aside, and regarding London with the cool or feverish eye of one intent on getting under its skin, it provides an endless fascination and feast for the senses.

Shocks there are aplenty for the first-time visitor, but not always of a repellent nature. From its ancient beginnings as the Roman town of Londinium to the present-day metropolis that socks you with its sassy, trendy, eclectic, decadent, dignified, historical and contemporary elements, London is the object of a universal fascination that transcends race, language, culture and social divides. Metropolitan London that is, not the urban fringes of Greater London that seem like pastoral Utopia compared to the seething heart.

Politics

London's government, without an overall elected metropolitan body, is unique in Europe. About half of the services are run by elected or indirectly elected bodies, with the rest run by central government or private companies. Life for the average Londoner is largely affected by which of the 30 boroughs he lives in. Local government, through the boroughs, is responsible for raising sufficient revenue for policing, education and social security services, road maintenance, hospitals, and local government itself. This has traditionally been funded by rates, a local property owning tax, abolished in Scotland in 1989 and in England and Wales in 1990 for the even more controversial community charge or 'poll tax' on every resident over 18 regardless of property or ability to pay. As of going to print, this taxation system is in turn under review, and a system more like the rating system is likely to replace it.

Different boroughs have different political compositions and different priorities on expenditure needs and hence on revenue needs. Thus it costs twice as much to live in Camden as it does in Kensington for instance. Yet, Kensington is a smart, upper-class area with handsome houses amid leafy avenues. And Camden is one of the dirtiest boroughs in London.

The People

More than a million Londoners (of the total eight million) belong to minority ethnic groups with the large majority coming from West Indian and Asian Indian stock. But unlike in New York, they are not ghetto-based, although immigrant and ethnic minority income levels tend to be low, so few blacks are found in Knightsbridge! Tension between the black community and the police does exist, and racial harassment, mainly by whites against Asian Indians, also remains a prickly problem.

Crime

It is far from comforting to know that you are more likely to be mugged in London than anywhere else in Britain. One in five major crimes committed in England and Wales and half of all the muggings take place in the Greater London area. Some 750,000 crimes are committed each year, by criminals as young as 12! Much is being done to combat this rising tide of violence. There are currently 66,000 neighbourhood watch schemes and 75 police divisions with a total workforce of 28,000. The former are very localised anti crime schemes almost exclusively in well off areas where there are tempting pickings for burglars, in which neighbours keep a close look out on their neighbours' properties and liaise frequently with local police officers in crime prevention. The good news is that there has been an overall drop in crime for the past few years.

Entertainment

London is arguably the best city in the world for entertainment, with as much variety as you can ask for. It is a major centre for the arts with the South Bank Centre as the world's largest arts complex. Four major orchestras, two opera houses, 65 cabaret venues and some 65 new plays every month make London an entertainment mecca. Not cheap, but far cheaper than in New York.

21

Parks

The city may be crowded, but London's green lungs make up for it. The Greater London area has 387 parks, 6000 acres (2400 hectares) of Royal Parks and 40,000 acres (16,000 hectares) of other parkland. For sports fans there are 70 major sports centres, 12 football league grounds, 30 running tracks, six ice rinks and 10 open air swimming pools.

Housing

Property prices that rocketed out of sight in 1988 are currently (1994) at an all-time low. Prices have dropped about 30% and investments have become negative equity for many people. Rents in London remain among the highest in the world but, despite this, even the grottiest, grubbiest room is snapped up within minutes of it being advertised.

Homelessness

An estimated 3000 people sleep rough anywhere they can find a warm spot and more than 20,000 are still in council-paid rented accommodation and hostels.

Pollution

London has earned the title of 'Dirtiest City in Europe' with the carbon monoxide level in Central London far exceeding WHO guidelines. A recent study by Oxford Polytechnic showed that some 45% of trees in Epping Forest are dead or dying from air pollution. Water pollution is also a growing cause for concern though it is still not known what the health effects might be.

Transport

Some 1.2 million workers commute to London every day, 450,000 by train, 400,000 by tube and 160,000 by car. There are 2.2 million London-registered cars with the average speed in Central London a crawling 11.5 mph (18.5 kilometres per hour)! The tube service is increasingly overused and overstretched, despite it being one of the world's largest and most complicated. It's also the oldest, most expensive and erratic! Government subsidies are low compared to most of Europe, with passengers meeting 84% of the costs; train commuters pay 29% in Milan and 34% in Paris.

Standard of Living
Londoners earn more than their counterparts in other British cities, but have to put up with a cost of living 36% higher than the national average. A family of four living in a three-bedroom house spends 40.5% more just to maintain a lifestyle comparable to that of a family in the north. London is bottom of the list where quality of life is concerned, with Scotland heading it.

Health
Despite having one of the best health services anywhere in the world, with a 1993/94 budget of £36 billion, 29 health districts and eight teaching hospitals, London's health provision is under constant heavy pressure. There is a hospital waiting list of some 140,000 people – up 40% since 1982. The National Health Service is entirely dependent on taxation but the government has, until recently, ignored public demands for more funding and resources. Hospitals are overcrowded, with services for the elderly and mentally ill in particular being chronically underfunded. Increasingly the well-to-do and those who can afford it are taking out private medical care schemes, so that routine operations can be done in private hospitals at their convenience and that of their employers. Emergency services remain free for all.

The Lure of London
But the millions still come to London as soon as the first shafts of the dawn light appear, drawn from the furthest corners of the globe. You reel from the first shock of lemming-like humanity moving about with desperate urgency to get somewhere; the push and shove

a herd-like instinct to answer some mysterious call. The streets, underground and pavements are a daily moving, bustling mass of people so intent on rushing that a strolling visitor is likely to be knocked off his feet.

As a magnet to consumers bent on purchasing the latest, the best, the trendiest or plain kitsch, and the gawkers lured here by the city's irresistible charm, London has infinite capacity to accommodate millions. Like a boardwalk of shifting scenarios, it provides an enthralling vista of diverse humankind rarely found elsewhere. Even among those who commute to London to work, the city is the object of a never-ending love-hate relationship for many.

In the space of a few minutes strolling through the West End – not merely the shopping precinct but the hedonistic pulse – you can capture a splendid rainbow of life. Women in *purdah*, Americans loudly demanding when the fog is due, European students chattering in a multitude of tongues, rich Japanese making a beeline for bespoke shops, vagrants, bag ladies, shifty-eyed, weasel-like men no doubt sizing up the day's purse-snatching potential, be-minked ladies of means, burger-munching back-packers – indeed it seems the whole world and a half are in London every day of the month.

The roar of ceaseless traffic is punctuated almost clockwork-like with screaming sirens of police cars heading for yet another crime spot. The pace is not for the faint-hearted nor diffident. Observation of the rat-like scurrying pace of passers-by can leave you breathless, let alone with enough presence of mind to take in other splendid features of London's architectural and historical treasures.

The Place

There are few places in the world that offer such an incredible juxtaposition of old and new, handsome and ugly, imposing and humble. A thousand years of history lie beneath the ancient streets, cobblestones, soaring edifices and traffic-snarled byways. While much building and refurbishing seems to go on ceaselessly, the heart of

Central London has the patina of centuries that provides reflective wonderment amid the shocks of the teeming masses. Surprises await the traveller at every other turn of the corner. Very much a walking city, the discovery of a quiet cul-de-sac – sometimes called a 'mews', originally an area of stabling now converted to chic housing – smack in the heart of a chrome, steel and smoked glass shopping area is sheer delight.

Ancient churches nestle among gnarled old oaks like oases of benediction among the cacophonous surroundings of car-strangled streets. Minutes from the main thoroughfares and you're into the green lungs of Regent's Park and Hyde Park that allow you to luxuriate in verdance away from noxious fumes.

Day-trippers, by the very nature of their urgency, rarely pause to reflect on this startling contrast. Taking in London through the lens of a camera robs most of the pleasure of this feeling. As a resident, I use London's green lungs as a much needed respite from the daily shocks of crushing humanity and beleaguered transport systems.

The West End

There is much here that offers more shocks per minute than anywhere else in Britain. Pushers, hookers, conmen are never far from your shoulder. But look not merely on this side of life but at the fascinating faces of the place, its handsome theatres, cinema halls, shops, pubs and facades that make the West End what it is. London is a unique collection of historical buildings, timeless squares, quaint arcades, high-tech and faded with age, gleaming glass and ancient pillars, grubby pavements and pristine cobblestoned alleys, shops rife with the atmosphere of a time past and soulless chain stores.

Within the little patch of land skirting the West End – Kensington, Bayswater, Paddington, Euston, Embankment, Westminster, Chelsea and Earl's Court – there is much that is entrancing, startling and mind-boggling.

Absorbing these places is an experience that touches most of the senses. Kensington is leafy, affluent and studded with handsome town houses even royalty would not be ashamed of living in. Kensington Palace is a museum of court dress where occasionally Prince Charles, Princess Margaret, Prince and Princess Michael of Kent and some lesser royals host functions of various types. Yet, within a stone's throw of these exclusive residences lies the roisterous, sleazy, cosmopolitan district of Bayswater that possibly has only a little less low life than that in Earl's Court. The former is actually better known for its ethnic restaurants and the latter for its street hookers and red light areas. Paddington seems more like a souk out of the Middle East with a plethora of kebab shops and Lebanese eateries. And there, but for the right turn of a corner, lies the wondrously green and peaceful Regent's Park.

Euston is a great maw of commercial buildings and railway stations, a source of bewilderment to visitors used, perhaps, to a more logical layout. Finding your way in and out of the bus, rail and train stations is an exercise to tax the heart and patience.

Embankment, Westminster and Chelsea are places you can walk into history. But it may come as a shock to see soaring steel and glass high-rises that seem rudely out of place next to the Houses of Parliament. This is a juxtaposition that has not sat well on conservationists, and the battle rages on.

The High Life

London's Belgravia abounds with sumptuous houses belonging to blue bloods, chief of whom is the Duke of Westminster who owns practically all of Westminster.

Most aristocratic homes (all over the country, not just in London) are open to the public for a small fee. This helps the families to maintain them. Many are heard to moan that it's a high price to pay, but the option is to ring for one's bank manager for a loan. So the high life still goes on where the family coffers and mansions are not in danger of insolvency. Millionaires abound in London but their flaunting of wealth speaks rather more of bad taste than impeccable lineage – something the British still set much store by.

The Low Life

The shock of seeing so many homeless, sleeping rough in London never quite leaves one. Thousands of disillusioned fortune-seekers, tearaways and the gullible are drawn to London in search of whatever it is they cannot find in their suburban or rural patch. Most find the streets are far from paved with gold – only the spectre of hunger and wretchedness. The authorities claim they are doing as much as they can but it is never quite enough. There are so many who have no direction, skills or ability to cope in a city that eats the down-and-out and spits them out, that the average Londoner, visitor or resident, usually has no time for them, being driven themselves to maintain their lifestyles. Horror stories of young boys and girls who end up as prostitutes and drug addicts are frequent.

It is not just youth who are so blighted in this sprawling city of so many faces where too few have time to care. There are thousands of old people, vagrants and bag ladies who wander the streets of London daily. Whatever the circumstances that have driven them to such degradation, there seems little hope of alleviating their depressing plights. In some cases, nothing can be done because they choose to live their shifting lives so. I have seen the same sad, hungry faces in the West End alleys huddling against the cold in filthy, threadbare clothes for years.

They rummage in garbage cans, clothe themselves with whatever they can find among the jetsam and are often lost in a haze of cheap alcohol. Drink appears to be a major cause but sociologists argue that they are driven to drink because of their miserable plights. Either they have no family, no home or have left welfare homes of their own volition. Whatever the reason, London's homeless are a sorry sight to see. One has only to be accosted frequently by young people, once robust with the bloom of youth and health now

27

reduced to piteous thinness, unhealthy pallor and filthy state begging for a few pence to realise the enormity of the problem.

The Ambience

Despite the grimmess of London's low life, the place has a special quality that can touch anyone to the core. A beholder does not have to be a poet to appreciate the multi-faceted nature of a metropolis that throbs and pulses to a thousand different beats. The exuberance of youth keeping up the frenetic pace of Piccadilly Circus; the seasoned mien of true Londoners seemingly untouched by the chaos as they down their pints of beer at quaint pubs; the splendour of St Paul's Cathedral and Nelson's Column dwarfing everything with their unbelievable majesty; the endless traffic choking every road, street and alley – these are a few of the many scenes that make up London's unique ambience.

Much of London's excitement lies not in the cash-for-flash genre but in the palpable aura of thrilling excitement; of simply being amid everything that is London. It costs nothing to stand, feel and hear the tingling resonance of Big Ben that seems to toll of times past. It costs nothing to feel the sense of medieval mores negotiating a cobblestone street between Tudor houses that seem to touch each other in closeness. Feel the heat of the Great Fire; smell the stench of the Plague.

If morbidity is not your cup of tea, fill your lungs with sharp air in the green parks of ever-changing floral displays. Or simply gaze at the splendid buildings that are divine examples of a flowering Renaissance centuries ago. Walking, seeing or taking in London needs singular concentration. A camera is for indelible mementoes but the mind is a much more permanent depository of all the things that make up London. The beautiful, ugly, sublime and ridiculous. To embrace the shocks is to feel for London what a thousand snapshots cannot do. To live with them and perhaps feel a sense of involvement can make London so much more welcoming. There are many who have recoiled from London perhaps having failed to do this. To be enamoured of London, once over the shocks, is to have a passionate love affair that can last a lifetime. To dislike London is to pass up a chance of life at a fast, frenetic, absorbing and utterly enchanting trot. Very few cities have this enigmatic appeal.

TAKE TIME OUT FOR LONDON

It is a mistake to try and take in London in a few days – even a few weeks – as it tends to be with visitors. When you plant your stakes here, and if you want to get to know London really well, allow at least several weeks, preferably months, of protracted walking and copious note-taking to do justice to your task.

Skimming the surface of any city is never satisfying – tourists are less concerned with in-depth knowledge than one-dimensional snapshots – more so with London than any other city. As I have mentioned, London is essentially a walking city.

Much of what's most interesting within metropolitan London is inaccessible by car, so you have to go on foot unless you're an avid cyclist; in that case, beware of the traffic. You take the tube and bus and then trudge to explore the nooks and crannies giving yourself ample time to savour everything. An old building is never just an old building. The story behind its walls makes a fascinating study in architectural history.

All these ramblings are an essential part of assimilating London if you are to feel a sense of belonging. Just like getting used to the train, bus and tube systems: they make for a much more meaningful stay. Champing at the bit when your bus is late does nothing for your mental equilibrium. Nor does it inculcate an indulgent fondness for London's idiosyncracies, of which there are many. For it is this that separates the London lovers from the haters. You learn to rise above irksome feelings about the tardiness, the crowding, pushing, shoving and lack of grace because they are an integral part of the great maw that is London.

29

Despite being one of the oldest in the world, the London Underground, commonly called the 'tube', is the best means of transport when you want to see as much of London as possible.

The Royal Albert Hall is simply breathtaking as an architectural curiosity – like a giant wedding cake. So is the much less somnolent Charing Cross Station. Both have their place in the complex heart that is London. Covent Garden – the covered market, that is, rather than the renowned and exclusive opera house – is brash, commercial and seemingly awash with tourists. But divorce your mind from the human multitude for a few minutes and cast it back to a time when it used to be a flower market that inspired *My Fair Lady*. Inigo

Jones – believed by some to be Britain's greatest architect – columns take on totally different perspectives and you almost feel the noise fading away, and Eliza Doolittle's cockney tones ringing round the corners.

Alternatively you can skim London's surface, whinge about the noise, shove and push and go away knowing as little as when you came. Take time to gather in the ambience of the surroundings, above the neon-lit brashness of present-day commercial enterprises and you'll discover a new love for the place. Not just as a sprawling tourist trap where porcelain knick-knacks are a cheap affront to the innate beauty of the place, but a place full of surprising charm and quaint beauty.

Above all, London cannot be rushed even if its very pulse seems to race with the wind. Give it time and you'll grow a fondness for it that makes up for all its shortcomings.

THE BRITISH PEOPLE

When Britannia was riding the waves and the 'Made in England' stamp had a definite prestige during the Industrial Revolution and right up till the 1960s, the Briton was as archetypal as his picture-postcard backdrop: the pudding-basin black bowler hat above a sober, stiff upper lip echoed by his tightly furled umbrella. His backdrop? Any one of the historical sights millions of tourists flock to Britain each year to gawk, photograph and marvel at. You can take your liberal pick from a Georgian mansion to an Elizabethan cottage, from Westminster Abbey to Canterbury Cathedral. This chocolate-box perfection was the arch lure for tourist revenue in untold millions.

Even as the scenario shifted with the times, this stereotype remained quintessential, an odd juxtaposition among the pearly kings and queens of cockney Britain, Teddy Boys, dolly birds, punks and country squires. Today, this image is seen as only reflective of some of the older and more traditional city commuters, all but drowned by the multitude of 80s imagery – the pop icons, trendy people and a multi-racial mix. A typical advertising poster might include an ethnic mix of people as representative of Britain today – not tokenism.

The origin of the British is rather more genetically mixed. They are descendants of the ancient Norman, Celtic, Saxon and Nordic tribes which settled here from 2000 BC until the 11th century.

Even before the Celts came, swarthy Mediterranean peoples had lived in Britain and founded cities like Canterbury and London. The Celts actually came 1000 years later – from Brittany in France and the Alps. Many moved north to Scotland and across the seas to Ireland, laying the foundation for the Irish and Scottish national parties which promote the revival of old Celtic languages.

The Cornish people still speak affectionately of their Breton cousins. Around 55 BC, the beady eyes of the Romans were cast on Britain and they conquered the Celts. However, the Roman empire collapsed during the 4th century falling prey to the newcomers – the Angles, Saxons and Jutes hailing from Germany. They in turn were conquered by the fierce Vikings who ruled by their blood-stained swords till the 11th century. William, the Duke of Normandy, with the help of Norman soldiers descended from Scandinavians, ascended the throne after the fateful Battle of Hastings in 1066.

Norman castles still dot the countryside. The Romans left their road systems, and ancient tongues pepper the spoken English today. Modern English emerged from a mix of Celtic, Norse dialects, Anglo-Saxon, Latin and Norman French.

By the early 19th century, Jews fleeing the pogroms of Eastern Europe flooded into Britain settling in the East London area of

Spitalfields. They prospered through the fur and clothing trade, and by the middle of the 20th century, another wave of immigrants moved in. Bangladeshis fleeing the poverty and strife of their crowded homeland stepped into the trades left by the departing Jews. A house of worship that still stands today in Brick Lane in East London reflects this demographic change. It was a French chapel dating back 300 years, then a Wesleyan church, a synagogue, and is now a mosque.

The Bangladeshis are themselves part of a larger community of people from the Indian sub-continent who began migrating here in the 1950s. Sikhs from the Punjab, Gujeratis, Ismailis and others from Kenya, Tanzania, Uganda and Malawi jostled for a living. They sought work in Leicester, Birmingham and other Midlands areas, moving later into London's Southall. Walking down the high street of this area evokes a palpable feeling of being in India.

From the 1950s too, West Indians came here in large numbers to take on jobs the British did not want – mostly menial and lowly paid. As Commonwealth subjects and regarding Britain as their mother country, they were not prepared for the shock of social rejection and often overt racial discrimination. Settling in the inner cities of London, Birmingham and Manchester, and working on railroads and other service industries, their lot was not a pleasant one, what with bad wages and anti-black feelings. Among the younger immigrants, anger became the common stance, often exploding in riots.

Citizens of Indian descent have become businessmen and professionals and some, together with those of Caribbean descent, now hold influential positions in the government. Britain today has a racial mix that reflects a global melting pot. The red hair description that Orientals are wont to give all British, indeed all Europeans, could not be further off the mark. There is no such thing as the average British national in terms of hair and skin colouring. One language is the common denominator.

Centuries of colonisation and immigration have turned British society into a very cosmopolitan one. Tolerance and respect for each other's cultures have helped many foreigners integrate fully into British society, though tension is never far from the surface in deprived areas.

However, there is a groundswell feeling of ethnic pride among the immigrants today. A minicab driver once told me he was Jamaican-born in England, but proudly Jamaican.

Didn't he like it here then? He is 20, working part-time to help pay his university fees and feels Britain is going to the dogs. It is a strong sentiment. When once their parents would have fought tooth and nail to remain in Britain, the second generation immigrants are rather ambivalent about their future in Britain. The common complaints are cost of living, overcrowding, perfidious racism and a general feeling of pessimism about the future.

It is not possible to categorise the British nation as a whole because you meet so many different psyches in relation to a foreigner in their midst. In areas where ethnic communities are thin and scattered, a sense of isolation can permeate as most English are slow to warm up to strangers, whatever their ethnic origin. The Welsh and Scots are generally more forthcoming. Visits up north confirm this. A Scottish friend often moans about the unfriendliness of his southern compatriots. Certainly, people in London – whether visitors or locals – seem less friendly than those in the counties and villages. This is mainly the result of the push-and-shove big city life and one can get sucked into this pattern unwittingly.

When you are among many of your own people, the tendency is to mingle almost exclusively among them, cutting against the grain of integration. Let us take a typical urban town in a county where there is a visible mix of English, blacks, Chinese, Greek Cypriots, Indians and other ethnic minorities. You live in a terrace house near the high street where kebab houses, pizza places, Chinese takeaways and Indian newsagents jostle with English supermarkets and West Indian greengrocers. An eclectic community that typifies many towns in Britain. The best opportunity to make friends and foster good relationships is via the trade. Business people are by design more forthcoming, cheery and less private. From here you build a certain foundation in the understanding of different cultures echoing

One place where you will make friends is at the greengrocer's. The street market also has a friendly atmosphere and the stallholders tend to be more garrulous.

much Britishness at the same time. I often shop at West Indian greengrocers that feature unusual produce not found in Chinese specialist stores and supermarkets.

Most shopkeepers warm up to regular customers but are loath to be too friendly for fear of being called nosy; unless you make the first move in striking up chumminess. There is a common ground to inter-relate with them if you take the first step. On home ground, poking your nose across the fence to make conversation is likely to elicit a certain reluctance to be friendly. Yet, the same person at the butcher or fishmonger will be more ready to engage in conversation over the relative merits of chicken or cod.

In many ways Britain's high streets of burgeoning ethnic shops and a growing interest in ethnic cuisines among even the conservative British have provided a conversational springboard. The same human bonds are less easily forged at department stores, bus stops and other public areas. Perhaps it is the fear of the unknown, here dispelled on the cosy ground of domestic routine. Somehow, picking, choosing and waffling over market produce creates an instant bonhomie; a conducive atmosphere that brings out the friendliest face of humanity.

WHO IS THE TRUE BRIT?
The Scots
The Scots are not all dour and are in fact very warm, extremely cultured and philosophical. As for being tight-fisted, it is an undeserved reputation. Who can generalise about such a personal trait? It is a sweeping statement at best and deeply offensive at worst, though the Scots are the first to make jokes about this national reputation – even on television. While self-deprecating, they are at the same time fiercely proud of their Scottish heritage.

The Welsh
Likewise, the Welsh will take umbrage if you should mistake them for English. A friendly, poetic and musical people, they join forces with the Scots to poke fun at the English. But then much of the basis of national humour takes a leaf from this free-for-all when someone takes a pot shot at another with tired old jokes by simply changing the nationality.

The Chinese
The Chinese from Hong Kong get incensed when referred to as 'Honkies'. Working with them can be skating on thin ice though many have been here for years or were born here. Perhaps they have been at the receiving end of bigotry from others envious of their diligence and financial acumen. But it's as well to be cautious. To

begin with, the Chinese are basically chauvinistic. As a result, many of them have never assimilated despite years of being British nationals. Many still harbour resentment, imaginary or otherwise, of being regarded as second class citizens despite having been in England for many years. It illustrates the different degrees of assimilation and how the inability to do so for whatever reason can be detrimental to a happy existence.

The Vietnamese

The Vietnamese are a new presence and still to make their attitudes felt. Mainly low profile, most are actually ethnic Chinese though the Chinese from Hong Kong for some inexplicable reason regard them with disdain.

Indians

Asian Indians are diligent, if unsmiling and rather clannish, preferring the company of their own kind. Many have opened their own corner shops, grocers or restaurants, and have become an accepted part of British life. Even small towns will have a late opening Asian Indian grocer often open seven days a week, upon whom residents rely increasingly for last minute purchases.

West Indians

The black West Indians are forthright and sometimes aggressive and speak their minds at whatever cost. You'll soon spot those with chips on their shoulders who see racism around every corner rightly or wrongly. Attitudes to work are different from those of Asian Indians, often a more 'laid back' approach to time keeping and reliability. Coupled with this, the West Indian community has a disproportionately high incidence of petty drugs – marijuana and the like – which in the case of the Rastafarian sect are part of their lifestyle and religion. Predictably such traits, together with a comparatively high crime rate in black areas, cause the (mainly white) police to view the West Indian community with suspicion and, sadly, frequent reports of wrongful arrests and harassment add to the tension.

Others

As for Canadians, Australians and Europeans, they're mostly upfront, easy going and fairly guileless. They are easy to get along with and, depending on personal philosophy, are much more immediately receptive to foreigners than British.

Again these are generalisations as it is impossible to pigeonhole any particular nationality. Every new resident in Britain must hone his instinct for human relationship and apply common sense, tact and maturity in forging a harmonious working rapport with the different nationalities. If you constantly cross swords with everyone

you meet or work with, it would seem you need to look within yourself. Do you perhaps harbour incipient bigotry? Are you oversensitive perhaps? Could you yourself be prejudiced if you seem to be the target of the same? Many bad vibes will dissipate when you clean up your act first.

WHAT ARE THE BRITISH LIKE?

Despite the pluri-ethnic population, and difficult though it is to generalise, there are traits common to most in the nation. Where they come from, whether country or urban, and their education and social backgrounds have a great bearing on their behaviour as a whole.

People from the counties and rural folk who live quieter lives are usually more polite, friendly and helpful when you ask for help. In the cities, especially London, a request for help does not always elicit warm response. More likely a brusque dismissal. Though this is true of most countries with highly urbanised city centres, public abrasiveness is particularly pronounced in a city that attracts more people than space would allow.

Likely as not, the person you ask for help is in a great hurry not to miss a train or tube and disinclined to waste precious minutes answering a query. Just as likely, he is a visitor who knows as little as you do. But by and large, the local Brits are helpful if you ask for assistance. They are not so ready to warm up though, if you ask too many personal questions. What might seem a normal query like "Which part of the country are you from?" will be construed as nosiness. When you get monosyllabic answers, leave off. Talk about the weather. It's the safest ground to break ice. The apparent lack of curiosity about other people is simply a greatly cherished sense of privacy and fear of invading yours.

The 'minding one's own business' syndrome has unfairly given the British an undeserved reputation for coldness. They are disinclined to make the first move, but when you do, you'll find the coldness thawing perceptibly – as long as you don't poke and pry.

41

Tradesmen in busy city centres are also likely to be offhand and brusque when approached for assistance. They are among the first people new arrivals meet, usually outside a railway station. You must understand that you are likely to be the 100th person to ask him where Buckingham Palace is. In the counties and suburban areas, people will go out of their way to direct you to a local attraction. For one thing, they don't get thousands of visitors every-day. For another, pride for one's local scene is deeply entrenched.

Silent Commuters

The British are notoriously tight-lipped during commuting, whether by train, tube or bus. When a train stops between stations for any reason, even for as long as half an hour, you can hear a pin drop. Few, apart from friends, are inclined to make casual conversation even as relief from the tedium of waiting. The only sound in a carriage of 30 people will be the rustling of newspapers. Visitors used to public bonhomie usually end up embarrassed when their remarks provoke only silence and weak smiles.

The occasional sight in tube trains of drunks and vagrants sing-ing and swearing would only make the British turn the other way and pretend this embarrassment is not there. The only people staring and smiling with bemusement are likely to be visitors.

THE LOCAL SOCIAL SCENE

If you've lived here long enough, or made enough effort to make friends among the locals, your social diary can be rewarding. It doesn't have to be whooping it up at nightclubs or doing the town. Relatively tame outings like sharing a car to drive out to the country, getting together to swap recipes and generally jaw a weekend away – these are the do's that make for easier, faster assimilation into the British mainstream of leisure activity. It is imperative that living among different races and nationalities, you'd want to be a part of their social calendar even if it's something alien to you at first.

When asked to join them at a pub, don't demur that you don't drink. It's more than having a drink – it's a national British pastime.

If asking neighbours over for a meal elicits no response initially, probably because they find foreign food offputting – and many British do – ask them in for tea. This is a social habit close to their own heart.

Basically the British are more than curious about foreign cultures and lifestyles, but do use subtle persistence to convince them you're totally sincere and do not expect any reciprocation. They are not inclined to hand out casual invitations to their homes and, for this reason, often refuse yours.

It is more than making nodding acquaintances across the garden fence. It's making the effort to convince the conservative, wary British that foreign residents, whatever their pigmentation, basically want to be accepted even if sometimes they don't quite understand the need for assimilation. When you meet a neighbour further afield and not sharing a common fence, a cheery good morning and cursory conversation about the weather and other light observations will widen your social register.

It's knowing what makes the British tick. The safe ice-breaking subjects are the weather, pets, gardens, children and their antics, community welfare– such as what to do about loud music from an unreasonable household – and problems that draw neighbours together to fight a common cause. It shows clearly that you care about the welfare of the community.

AT WORK

The office you work in will probably have a large proportion of British staff, so make a supreme effort to be on their wave length. Office procedures all over the world are quite similar, but you can look into their culture in a number of ways, for example by sharing their lunch pattern. British workers often have a rather simple lunch routine: while factories and industrial units may have a workers' canteen serving a complete, carbohydrate-full lunch or dinner, for many workers, sandwiches and soft drinks augmented by chocolate bars are the order of the workaday week.

Joining in local lunch arrangements will repel the likelihood of (a) isolating yourself in an all British environment and (b) winning your colleagues over with your genuine keenness to share your culture. Convincing them that you're an anglophile is not the best way to win British friends either. The British have a healthy regard for aliens who preserve their own culture and at the same time have a healthy curiosity about theirs. It endorses the fact that you are not a passenger among their midst and nothing demystifies the 'inscrutable' or insular tag more than when you show cursory knowledge of British culture. It can become an invaluable cue for the Brit to break out of his rigid reserve and tell you all you want to know. Be it the best way to brew a cup of tea or which pub has the best ale.

Even if the organisation you work in has a reputation for being egalitarian and anti-racist, the balance of minority ethnic working among the majority of British can be fragile. Curtail your hypersensitivity about the jokey peccadilloes that might come your way. Innocent ribbing is a good basis to form warm working relationships if you don't read any more into it. Unless you know for sure it was said with real venom, take it in the right spirit of cheeky ragging. Incidences of outright racism within a working environment are relatively rare and, if they persist, take the matter up with the proper authorities.

OF LAUGHTER AND LAMENT

Strange bedfellows, yet the slight paradox of being custodian of a jut-jawed stiff upper lip and a wry sense of humour is very British. Here, there must be some qualification as Scottish, Welsh and English people each have their own laughter medicine. Fundamentally, all have a similar self-deprecating sense of humour that is refreshing. It's often bandied about that if Americans laughed at themselves more often, they wouldn't spend so much time on a psychiatrist's couch. Supposed national characteristics are woven into the jokey pattern – Scottish meanness, Welsh romance and English coldness.

It's humour that's pervasive, spilling out over just about every aspect of life. You'll notice that most British advertisements, whatever the selling message, usually have a tongue-in-cheek touch. You'll be hard put to meet a nation more ready to laugh at themselves. Brought up as I was on absolute filial piety, rapping with my elders was simply not done. Here, I have met many elderly friends who are uproariously funny and not afraid to show it. Naturally, in the beginning I was most reluctant to say anything that might be regarded as impudent. But they soon put me at ease with their cracking good humour, some positively blue!

The great British put-down, as they say, is almost always aimed inwards and you see this more markedly on stage and television than anywhere else.

In the characterisation of a drab person, replete with curlers in the hair and bedraggled clothes, no punches are pulled. This is something you don't often see on American TV where glamour is all – full make-up in bed, etc. In fact, this sense of honesty has enshrined many characters as national symbols – the charlady forever in her pinafore, the tramp, the frumpy housewife, the henpecked husband, etc. – not just as fiction, but a reflection of real life.

Nothing is sacred when it comes to squeezing a laugh. Not politicians, royalty or even the priesthood. Anyone taking offence at being the target of jokes (as long as they are not libellous) is soon despatched with even more razor barbs and regarded as insufferable. In the TV programme *Spitting Image*, rubber puppets of the most famous faces are stretched to lugubrious lengths. The Queen, for instance, is seen as the quintessential English woman with a tiara over her dowdy scarf and mouthing the most plummy tones. In a more restrictive society, what the producers of the programme do could land them in jail – but not in Britain. Anyone is fair game as a butt for jokes and you can only laugh along – or curl up and die.

As for the other face of the British psyche, the indomitable spirit not to break down in the face of disaster is most admirable.

You read often about tragedy – the litany in the past two years includes the Zeebrugge ferry, the King's Cross fire, the Piper Alpha oil rig, the Lockerbie plane crash – where aggrieved families rarely show anything but the bravest, stoic faces. It's a trait you see again and again where people touched by tragedy prefer to bite their lips in public than crumble in a heap. Carrying on regardless is what they call it – as epitomised in the hilarious series of British comedies regarded as classics of British mores.

Making a scene is not being British at all, which also explains why you rarely see them complaining about bad service. If a customer is upset about anything, he will not make a public fuss. He will make a polite comment and leave it at that. Consumer watchdogs in the past few years have been getting at the British public for this reticence to complain, thus perpetuating the bad service.

Whether it's good or bad is not the point here. If you were to become vociferous about some injustice, you would get the feeling you were being uncivilised by the curious looks of other customers. It is a good thing when you can complain without histrionics as you often see in other societies not given to the same diffidence.

This understanding of their psyche is important if you are never to feel at odds among British people. Nor should you take offence when they make jokes about you for it is meant to be taken in this light. If anyone were to be deliberately vicious, racist or otherwise rude, he wouldn't bother to make a joke of it. Learn to take it in the same spirit and you'll find them warming up to you as a mate. Indeed, one of the best compliments you could be paid is to be regarded as a mate.

– Chapter Three –

A BABEL OF SOUNDS

The English language evolved from a babel of Celtic, Anglo-Saxon, Latin, Norse and Norman French dialects. The untrained ear to this linguistic mix would be hard put to tell the difference between a Scots accent and an Irish one, both having similar 'burrs'. Being a largely monolingual country, Britain is at least comforting for anyone who reads and writes the language, no matter how rudimentary. How much English you should know in order to feel comfortable is a rather difficult barometer. Suffice that you should be able to read road signs, bus, tube and train schedules which have the basic destination/times/frequency/routes information. Obviously being able to speak basic English is a must; otherwise you are likely to feel isolated. It doesn't stop one from shopping at supermarkets and department stores as they are largely self-service and you simply pay what is rung up without any need for conversational exchange. Again, it all depends on your livelihood, where you work and who you need to relate to. Many foreigners, Chinese, Cypriot, Indian, etc, have got by for decades knowing barely six words of English. It makes the difference between feeling perpetually alien and at home. Few English find the need to learn a second language – a recent survey showed that 90% of students drop French by the time they do their O-level exams at age 15 or 16 – and they generally feel that anyone who lives here has a duty to learn English. Which is a practical attitude as the whole structure of society is based on one language.

With a common Europe looming, most language institutes are doing a thriving trade as much for Europeans to master English as for the English to master one or the other of the EC languages. Outside the specific need for a foreign language, say in the travel or European banking industry, the British are justifiably complacent about being monolingual. It is always useful to know more than one language but the fact is that, in England, simply knowing English is quite enough. Nor do the English see the need to learn Chinese or Gujerati or Thai as second and third generation foreigners are totally at home with the local language after years of immersion in English schools where, at best, a few hours are devoted to a second language. As for the immigrant languages, British education authorities believe that it is best left to the individual parents.

ACCENTS FIRST

Accents can vary so much that you may wonder what languages you are hearing. Whichever gateway you choose to enter Britain, your ears will be immediately assaulted by the dozens of regional accents. This is more so in London than in any other port or city. And to make you even more confused, you will hear quite a few hybridised accents, the result of being wrapped around migrant tongues. Like a Punjabi speaking broad Scottish or a Vietnamese lilting Yorkshire. Standard English is increasingly getting muffled amid the babel; it is only audible among the better educated. Even street conversation sounds alien to the ear untuned to the multiple nuances of a monolingual base.

Standard English pronunciation is not typical of any particular area of the country, but is more an indication of the level of general education and wealth. Thus residents of the richer counties near London will often speak with plummy accents, and originally the BBC – British Broadcasting Corporation – conformed to this standard. Nowadays there is a revival of interest in local dialects and using regional pronunciation is not an indication of a lower status.

The reason for this change is that it is the language of the people. Which perhaps explains why most state schools have not put too much emphasis on Standard English for years. On TV and radio programmes, the norm is to juxtapose the different regional accents – in short it is not *de rigueur* any more for the announcers to sound uniform.

With so much population diffusion and movement related to work, specific speech patterns tend to be restricted to small groups. Within an office, the managing director could very well have risen from the ranks, to lock his cockney vowels with the junior executive's public school consonants.

In Victorian times, language separated the classes with a fine divide. The division is less strict today though it still exists. And in these very same great houses that are now bed and breakfast places or divided into birdcage size flats, language is a mash of different accents with the occasional plum.

With so much diffusion of working population and migrant second and third generation peoples freed from the need to be within their ethnic enclaves, most major cities in Britain are a veritable jumble of linguaphone tapes gone mad.

Not surprisingly, a few European and Asian children born in Britain retain some of their mother tongue accents. You soon learn to spot the son of a Mauritian-born woman or the daughter of a Gujerati merchant. The characteristic sing-song lilt of Mauritian English and the 'yindian' accent are unmistakable. This again depends on how much the peer group influence is. Your linguistic hurdle can be sinister or simply quaint, depending on who you meet first. The immigration officer's probing tone is frightening enough without your having to translate his strange vowels into intelligible English. You should simply say, "Would you speak slowly, sir, I cannot understand you," and he will be more helpful. He is highly suspicious of anyone who does not speak English, never mind that you don't understand his.

After getting past this forbidding civil servant, you will be assailed by the more raucous – and initially unintelligible – tones of a cockney taxi driver. Both speak English but they could be from different planets. Still, the taxi driver would regale you with the story of his life, the current political disorder or the vagaries of British weather.

Just emit the occasional "uh-huh" and he'll thank you profusely when you tip him, as you should, about 10% being the standard practice here.

It has taken me eight years to distinguish between the soft lilt of the Yorkshireman, the clipped burr of the Scotsman and the strangeness of Liverpudlian which, at first, sounded positively Germanic! English as you have been taught completely disappears.

Actors have been known to spend years at speech classes to iron out their tongues, even to bury their oral origins so as to deliver their lines with thespian panache. Or at least clear enough to reach the furthest stall seat. After being orientated, I found it an absolute delight to sit through two hours of pure cockney in the West End musical *Me and My Girl*.

WHAT, RATHER THAN WHERE

From banks to beauticians, from schools to super-markets, your ears will be assailed with what seems like a dozen different tongues. Never mind where they originate, it's what they mean that's important if you are to assimilate into the British life.

The groundswell feeling is that regional accents should not be derided but preserved and perpetuated. Gone is the belief that to get places, you have to speak properly. Several days of watching British television will soon endorse this. The day is yet to come when the national News, that fount of media articulation, goes regional though some weathermen on TV are barely intelligible at first to the foreign ear, and regional news programmes are generally presented with regional accents.

Street English

'Butter' is pronounced with the Ts all but gone, replaced by a glottal stop − 'ba-er'. Or if your name is 'Peter', don't be miffed when someone calls you 'Pee-er'.

A favourite tag phrase among many is the quaint 'Know wot oy maen?' It seems a polite poser to the recipient of such accented English and so universally known it even comes on TV advertise-ments. A definite plus for keeping taproot language alive.

A 'nipper' is also a small child and 'tatty' could be a potato rather than your cut-price decor. A 'moggy' is the affectionate name for a cat and many grandmothers are called 'nans'. The epitome of an English parlour scene is someone's 'nan' cradling her 'moggy' on her lap while waiting for her kettle to boil to make a 'cuppa' (tea).

The list is far too long to chronicle here (see *Colloquialism* below) but don't be diffident about asking someone what he means when a word seems alien. Not that explanation will enlighten you any further, but it's the start of better communication when you have to explain your own language peculiarities.

51

Colloquialism

The dictionary definition of 'conversational idiom' does little justice to this rich patois of the people. With a definite penchant for oversimplification, they top it with sheer inventiveness. Possibly the Australians fare a close second in the alternative stakes. After all, they inherited most of their speech semantics from the British, giving it a twist only Crocodile Dundee can deliver with some panache.

A 'quid' is a pound. Small change is 'coppers' and a 'copper' is a policeman or a bobby. To 'come a cropper' is to fall down or get into trouble, for instance if you've 'nicked' a copper or two from someone's open handbag. To 'nick' is to steal and 'nosh' is food. You can get 'knackered' just thinking about it. Or exhausted if you prefer. If your car or house is 'in good nick', it needs no repair.

'Wonderful, innit?' Isn't it? Or is it not? if you prefer Shakespeare. A 'prezzy' is a present and a 'prat' is someone who's plain obnoxious. Especially when he lurches at you 'pie-eyed and legless', too drunk to get his knees up or to party.

When someone is 'chuffed', he's happy and pleased. When something is 'naff', it is very unstylish, almost embarrassing to be associated with. This particular word has its salty use when the situation demands. 'Naff off' is a polite version of that favourite Anglo-Saxon dismissive term not generally used in polite company.

Rudeness, it seems, is excusable as long as the rude word or term is masked over with another one usually found in respectable dictionaries. In fact more and more of these words and terms are sneaking into the best of almanacs.

'Bonkers' means mad, but 'bonking' is now acceptable, even on TV, though it is a word that describes the sexual act. It is now so acceptable – perhaps as a valve for verbal frustration – you could use it in front of your nan and she wouldn't ask you to naff off. A 'nerd' is a term of abuse really meaning a person who is ungainly, rather fumbling and incompetent. It is more generally used in 'you nerd' if a person does something silly or idiotic. There was recently a whole West End play called *The Nerd* about a man who was a born loser in life.

When someone says he's 'thick as two planks', it's self-deprecatory mocking of his mental capabilities. And to be 'thick and wet' – well, there must be air between the ears. Or an air-head. Or simply plain stupid. Or you've got nothing for a 'noggin' – brains.

And when asked to 'sod off', you can either take offence or not, depending on the tone of voice and who is issuing this dismissal. This is the saltier, less polite dismissive akin to the other word 'naff', as in 'naff off'. Both take their cue from that famous four-letter Anglo-Saxon word. Sod, by the way, is an abbreviation of Sodom.

It appears colloquialism has been invented so that refined society can let off steam without blurring the meaning of their vocal intention. It in fact has laid a fine film over obscenities, allowing even little old ladies to indulge in occasional swearing without turning a blue-rinsed hair.

There's something to be said for a language that can be used to convey displeasure without ensuing fisticuffs. Not surprisingly, it has given the British a reputation for biting sarcasm, sardonic put downs and other verbal killers. The dreadful alternative employed among the 'yobos' – now there's a descriptive idiom – is the repetitive use of that famous four-letter word.

'Yob' is boy spelt backwards and generally refers to unruly and uncouth males, some of whom make it their sole ambition in life to get as drunk as often as they can afford to while tearing around the country appearing to support their football team but in reality making a right nuisance of themselves. This problem multiplied a thousand fold became a national headache. The yobo sub-culture is a real social disease, spreading its scruff-bag, pie-eyed philosophy right across to Europe – mainly Spain. Some European authorities have begun to ban those undesirables.

There was a time when youthful enthusiasm for life and all it had to offer resulted in no more than some hot-in-the-head lad being called 'Jack the lad'. As portrayed by Michael Caine in the classic *Alfie*. This term is somewhat antiquated and turns up so frequently that it actually reflects a virtue compared to the mayhem created by the other lot. Alas, choice idiom or epithet cannot stem causeless rebellion and the advice is, when confronted with such characters on the street, tube, train or building site, refrain from using any. Just go away or report to the police if you are physically manhandled.

As well as a wide range of colloquialisms, some of which have been outlined here, you may come across the impenetrable Cockney Rhyming Slang. A couple of examples will show its wry sense of humour: the telephone is the 'dog and bone' ('bone' rhymes with 'phone') and the wife is 'trouble and strife'.

It's not just individual words that floor foreigners. Jargon is made even more garbled with terms of reference largely alien to the rest of the English-speaking world.

Trying to find accommodation through the classifieds is a protracted exercise in decoding that by the time you make any sense of it, you are too late. Try this: 'Rm, ch, bt entr in des. res. off st pk.' Room, central heating, basement entrance, in desirable residence, off street parking.

TOUCH

On the pleasant side of physical contact, the British are generally free of taboos that beset others, especially Orientals who don't like any kind of overt physical gestures.

With a first time acquaintance, a firm handshake is in order whatever your gender, though young people, especially teenagers and yobos, would find this too formal. On knowing someone a little better – some may call it affectation but it's regarded as refinement among many British – a peck on the cheek is acceptable. Male and female of course.

Many Europeans kiss both cheeks resoundingly and across all gender. The British way is very restained, more the woman proferring her cheek with a slight tilt of her head so the man may gently touch it with his cheek at the same time making a puckering sound.

PARK BENCH INTRODUCTIONS

This is one of the best ways to communicate with a Briton: he's already in the right and receptive frame of mind basking in the sun. There is no other reason (or time) to sit on a park bench. Talk about the weather is the usual ice breaker but don't ask nosy questions like where he or she works, lives or salary earned. Even among close acquaintants, such topics are deemed too personal. I know many British friends who have never mentioned what they do, and very few would dream of mentioning how much they earn. Money is generally a taboo subject: you should not ask how much people have paid for purchases.

Once in a while you will meet a jolly old soul, a bit worse for drink, who'll tell you everything including the size of his belly button. There are thousands of lonely old people in Britain who long for some sort of social contact and, on a nice day, a park bench is the best stage for dispelling woes. I used to be slightly annoyed when someone persisted in making conversation – having learnt to respect the British sense of privacy – amid the waft of alcoholic breath. Humour these people because often a few kind words can give a lift in their otherwise dreary lives.

HELPING THE BLIND

It's an automatic reaction to want to reach out to help a blind person when he or she seems lost, tap-tapping with regulation white stick. The blind in Britain are fiercely independent, having been trained to be so, and have a sixth sense more developed than most of the five in sighted people. They are not as helpless as they seem and if they have a routine of travelling to and from work on public transport,

55

they know exactly where to get on and off. Offer your help verbally by telling them what train is arriving, especially lines with different branches forking off at some point. Blind school instruction teaches them to be wary of strangers offering physical assistance as there are too many cases of the blind being robbed and mugged. So don't be offended if a blind person shrugs off your arm because he'd rather be safe than sorry.

SIGN LANGUAGE

Certain TV programmes and news bulletins have an interpreter using sign language and sub-titles for the benefit of the deaf. Hearing aids are obtainable from the National Health Service and most partially deaf will have had one fitted, so don't shout when talking to someone you know to be hard of hearing.

Chapter Four

A HISTORICAL PERSPECTIVE

Throughout the centuries, the history of Britain has been inextricably linked with religion. It is significant that the head of the Anglican Church is the head of state, that is the Queen.

THE CHURCH OF ROME AND THE BEGINNING OF PROTESTANTISM

Britain was annexed by the Roman Empire in AD 44 and after Christianity became the state religion of Rome in the 4th century, it began to spread rapidly. Rome, Catholicism and Britain flourished together until AD 410. However Britain was left alone to fight off the marauding Scots and Picts from up north. By the 6th century, the defenders had established political power and the next six decades saw the growth of Roman Catholicism in Kent, Sussex, Essex, Wessex, East Anglia and Northumbria.

By the time of the Plantagenets, the Anglo-Norman state was all powerful. Henry II consolidated his power, made great reforms and established the common law system. This was the beginning of the strain between Crown and Church. His archbishop, Thomas à Becket, was fiercely against his policy of punishing clerics for their involvement in secular matters, and was murdered by four royal knights on the altar at Canterbury in 1170.

When Henry died, his son Richard (The Lion-heart) took the throne only to spend most of his time in crusades abroad. His brother John's subsequent corrupt rule caused open revolt among the church barons but their plans to seize political power were destroyed by the Pope.

When John's son, Henry III, took the throne, feudal England was undergoing much upheaval. The king was beginning to lose his absolute power as Head of the Realm. By the time of his son Edward I's rule, England was a reformed nation with cohesion between Crown and Church. This was the era of great Christian buildings, at Lincoln and Salisbury and Westminster in London. More strife beset the nation after Edward I's death. His bungling son Edward II lost Scotland to Robert Bruce at the Battle of Bannockburn in 1314. Baronial anarchy was largely suppressed during the subsequent reign of his son Edward III who died in 1377 and his grandson Richard II became king. Henry, the Duke of Lancaster, was eyeing the throne and, in the ensuing decade of plot and counter plot, killed Richard and proclaimed himself Henry IV in 1399. From then until Tudor times in 1485, England was ravaged by religious and political intrigue. Henry Tudor began to squeeze the Church for more money to fund his royal wars as Rome's influence dwindled. The Church was discredited and monks began to lose their discipline.

The more puritanical reacted against this laxity but the Church was still all-powerful and Cardinal Wolsey was the most feared churchman in England. He lived on a lavish scale in Hampton Court and controlled what was effectively the gateway to all professions. Resentment grew until the 1517 Reformation took place in what is now Germany. Henry VIII was obsessed with producing a male heir and when his first wife Catherine of Aragon bore him a daughter, his eyes soon fell on one of her ladies-in-waiting, Anne Boleyn. His request for a divorce was rejected by Rome and he passed a series of anti-clerical acts with the backing of the Reformation Parliament.

He also appointed his lawyer, Thomas Cranmer, as Archbishop of Canterbury who then annulled his marriage to Catherine and had her daughter Mary declared a bastard. Anne, meanwhile, gave birth to a girl, Elizabeth. The incensed Pope nullified Cranmer's annulment and excommunicated both. In retaliation, Henry decapitated Thomas More his Chancellor who refused to fall in with his plans, appointed Thomas Cranmer to the Privy Council and declared himself Supreme Head of the English Church.

He dissolved the monasteries, seized their vast landholdings and decapitated Anne for failing to produce a son. He married Jane Seymour who died bearing him the future King Edward VI. Cromwell introduced Protestantism into the English Church, and infuriated Henry so much he too lost his head in 1540. When Henry died in 1547, his enormous kingdom was expanding hugely but his son, the boy king Edward VI, was incapable of ruling.

When he died, his half-sister, Catherine of Aragon's daughter Mary, acquired the throne. A devout Catholic, she restored the Church to its former power, re-installed the bishops and began to close ties with Rome once again. In her brief reign she committed genocide in the name of Catholicism. But Mary was childless and when she died, Elizabeth, Anne Boleyn's daughter, seized the throne, thus ending the Catholic insurgence once and for all. She ruled for 45 years with sensible moderation. The new Puritans who had fled to the continent during Mary's reign returned. The English Church became more reliant on private interpretation of scripture, rather than ritual and episcopacy.

By the time James VI of Scotland became King James I of England, Scotland and Wales, there was tremendous pressure from Scottish Presbyterians. The sect had evolved from 'presbyteries' – local councils of elders under the authority of a synod who had no time for bishops and Anglican rituals.

Other Protestants clamoured for reform along the Scottish lines, demanded more say in the government and persisted in purifying the Anglican Church with its 'popish' rituals, ceremony and priestly pomp. The Catholics also began to push for a return to the old papacy of Mary. James I died in 1625 with his realm still in turmoil over religious, political and financial differences. His son Charles I had Catholic tendencies but was a weak politician. He hid behind the Archbishop of Canterbury and together they set out to halt Protestant reforms in his infamous Eleven Years of Tyranny. The demands became even more revolutionary and, by 1642, England erupted into civil war. The royal army was routed by Oliver Cromwell, a member of the Parliament that Charles had imperiously ordered dissolved.

The country was now in chaos and in 1649, Cromwell had Charles beheaded for treason. His son fled to France in exile. England was now effectively ruled by Parliament, fumblingly. Cromwell sacked the members and replaced them with his churchmen. This Parliament of Saints elected him Lord Protector in 1653.

He died leaving the chaos in the hands of his son Richard. The exiled Charles II seized the opportunity to overthrow the incompetent Richard and restored the monarchy in 1660.

But the throne's power was now at its lowest ebb, though the Church of England was restored. When the Great Fire of London razed the city in 1666, it gave Sir Christopher Wren the opportunity to rebuild the great religious edifices. St Paul's Cathedral stands in magnificent testimony. Charles began to lean favourably towards the Catholics again, to the fury of Parliament. His brother, James, was a devout Catholic and heir to the throne. Catholicism was once again rearing its head in 1678 but before Charles could consolidate his efforts to stave off the threat, he died leaving the throne to the Catholic James.

In the Glorious Revolution, Protestants installed the Dutch William and his wife Mary Stuart in 1688. In his hatred for the French, William involved England in wars with France that lasted well into the reign of Anglican Queen Anne.

Many rebellions were to follow for the next few decades and 18th century Britain saw much wealth and flowering of the arts. Cities mushroomed, the East India Company and the Bank of England accumulated vast resources, the result of hard-working precepts laid down by the earlier Puritans.

The two revolutions between 1740 and 1780 were neither religious nor political. They were the Agrarian and Industrial revolutions which had great impact on Britain for hundreds of years to come. James Watt invented the steam engine, John Wilkinson invented new uses for iron and the country saw a burgeoning of building, manufacturing and farming. The old Puritan values of thrift and hard work became the national ethos. Children working 16 hours a day were a common plight. The Anglican Church did little to help these wretched people. In fact, Anglicanism seemed to have burrowed under ground.

Wesley gave endless sermons about man's sublimation to God, the Methodism for selfless labour and thrift. At least he died leaving his religious belief as spiritual uplift for the lot of the miserable factory hands.

Religious ferment was kept under wraps while Britain pursued commercial, industrial and colonising aims. But the American colonies began to champ at the bit and proclaimed themselves independent after the 1783 victory. The Methodists, who supported the

American cause, began to stir the lower classes. They had in fact caused an anti-Catholic riot in 1780.

The next three decades were to see Europe in bloody turmoil again. The French Revolution of 1789 had the English aristocracy quaking in their satin boots and lacy jabots. Louis XVI lost his pompadoured head, Napoleon Buonaparte was a blood-thirsty little general and it was Horatio Nelson who began to turn the tide in 1804 with his spectacular victory at Trafalgar. His statue now takes pride of place above his soaring column in London's Trafalgar Square. Napoleon was finally defeated at Waterloo by Arthur Wellesley, the Duke of Wellington.

Midway through Queen Victoria's reign, murmurs of church reforms began to surface. The Oxford Movement wanted a return to the ritual of Anglican service which had languished for the last hundred years. The Puritan dissenters began to push for their own churches. Quakers, Congregationalists, Baptists, Presbyterians and Methodists did not want to conform to the Church of England. Reforms by 1833 were to have far-reaching effects. The religious intensity of Christian socialism was aimed at bettering the lot of women and workmen's colleges.

Today

The Church of England – its members are called Anglicans – has kept certain marks of its previous Catholic identity. The church has bishops headed by the Archbishop of Canterbury and his deputy, the Archbishop of York, who under them have 40 assistant bishops. There are 69 dioceses, each with 200 parishes, and every parish is under the religious leadership of a priest. He may be called a rector or a vicar, all of which mean the same thing.

Bishops are appointed by the Queen from nominations presented to the Prime Minister. The bishop lives from the donations of his congregation and a stipend from the central church. Financial matters are handled by church commissioners.

The Church of England is one of Britain's major land owners and all church expenditure comes from this revenue. It also has 18,700 church buildings to maintain, which takes a big chunk of the income for many of them are hundreds of years old and require not only constant care but delicate refurbishing. The Church of England is not funded by the state, though it is ultimately answerable to Parliament and cannot legislate without Parliament's sanction.

Foreigners exposed to English literature have come across the vicar most frequently, and perhaps labour under the misconception that only sleepy villages have vicars. Witness the Agatha Christie mysteries that invariably have a vicar popping up somewhere. But urban cities also have vicars who preside at public worship.

Most parishes have an Anglican church, some two, depending on the size. An Anglican vicar is licensed by the state to perform marriages, baptism and funerals – in short he is the local community shepherd. He's also sometimes known as the parson. Marriage ceremonies in other denominational churches are attended by a state functionary, or preceded by a registry office ceremony, since it is only the Church of England that is licensed in this way.

You often hear reference to High Church which implies the type of service and not, as you may think, a class distinction or architecture. A High Church service can be elaborate with ceremonial use of vestments, incense and candles as opposed to a simple one with the minimum of trappings.

RELIGIOUS BRITAIN

Cynics might say – and they're backed in no small measure by church leaders – that this is a misnomer. There has been a general decline in Christian faith and church attendance in Britain over the past decades. This can be attributed to many factors: breakdown of extended families, moral laxity and general disillusionment brought about by unemployment and urban stress. The rising tide of secularism is very real according to Dr John Cullen, Director of the Insti-

You will come across all types of churches in Britain, from the little country chapel in a tiny village to awesome cathedrals which tower imposingly over one whole city.

tute of Christian Studies in London, "People are suspicious of church practices and the hide-bound philosophies therein. They find it difficult to relate Christianity to their daily life."

Whatever the religious inclinations of British people, thousands of churches and cathedrals built over a thousand years still stand in magnificent testimony to the Christian faith, attendant upheavals and bloody wars in the name of Christ.

Visitors from non-Christian countries and those with minimal Christian communities will be awed by the well-preserved antiquity and grandeur of these historic buildings. Places of worship they may be but, as tourist attractions, they lure millions of people to gasp and gawk, and perhaps to pray.

That this patronage helps to fund the religious organisations running their churches is undeniable. Each is run with efficiency, giving visitors comprehensive information about its history and service schedules. The architectural beauty and ecclesiastical ambience of Christian churches in Britain provoke different reactions in different people. If your inclination is to reach for your camera, check first to see if photography is allowed.

Apart from those that are in ruins, standing only by the grace of God and the preservation council, churches and cathedrals are first and foremost places of worship. The unending queues of tourists with fingers poised on cameras can be a headache to church elders trying to conduct services. Service times are usually listed on the door outside the main chapel together with information on what areas are out of bounds and whether photography is permitted.

It would be disrespectful to flout any of these, remembering that, whatever the tourist attraction, the church remains a sacred place. This fundamental observance must also apply to all religious places, even a heap of ancient stones where a church stood centuries ago. All over Britain can be found such founts of religious practice, pagan and Christian. Each is sacrosanct and must not be sullied by littering, graffiti or uncivil regard.

Don't simply traipse through clicking at every architectural detail and marble sarcophagus. Where a church has had a particularly long and interesting history, an area will be designated for visitors to browse and soak up the unravelling story via pictures and text.

Ecclesiastical postcards, religious artefacts and other literature are on sale at many churches and cathedrals of a certain age and historical import. It's one of the best ways of boning up on British history that for hundreds of years was inextricably entwined with Christian evolution.

More pertinent to the foreigner is an understanding of British Christian history and the terms of references used in the community.

In 1990 total church membership in the United Kingdom was 65%, with active church membership at Trinitarian churches – those believing in the Holy Trinity in unison with God – a mere 14%, or 6.7 million people. Of these 1.82 million were Anglican, 1.95 million Roman Catholic and 2.92 million of other Protestant denominations. Membership of non-Christian religions has more than doubled from 1975 to 1990, with 1.74 million active adherents in 1990, the largest group being Muslim.

Great Churches

There are far too many to list, this being a random pick of the more handsome and better-known examples.

Westminster Abbey and St Paul's Cathedral, both in London, may have become the best-known symbols of tourist and religious Britain, but are by no means the most grand.

Westminster Cathedral, in Victoria, is a Roman Catholic church built in 1890 in a rather eclectic style reminiscent of Byzantine and Italian styles. The Anglican church of St Martin's-in-the-Fields, built in the early 18th century, became the prototype of dozens of others in New England in America.

As for St Paul's, it rose out of the ashes of 1666 London after the Great Fire had razed the city to the ground. Its Italian baroque reflects St Peter's in Rome, but was, and still is, dedicated to the Protestant faith. It is the venue for most regal ceremonies, Princess Di and Prince Charles' wedding for one.

Wessex is known for its twin offerings of Winchester and Salisbury Cathedrals – both dating back to Norman times.

Not far from these is the mystical Stonehenge; the purpose for which the stones were erected remains a fascinating mystery. Believed to be the site of pagan sun worshipping by the ancient order of Druids, it still draws modern day druids by the thousands each Midsummer Day.

Canterbury is the cradle of English Christianity and the cathedral drew many pilgrims for centuries. It was built largely between 1100 and 1400 with some parts dating back to AD 602. Its stained glass windows alone are worth a visit. Dotted all over the countryside are remains of Roman ruins and St Augustine's College near the ruins of its ancient abbey today trains Anglican clergy.

Exeter Cathedral is Devon's most imposing building in the West Country. Built between the 11th and 12th centuries in Norman Gothic style, it has the largest surviving group of 14th century sculptures in England. Among its treasures are the 14th century Bishop's Throne and the Exeter Book of Old English Verse.

York Minster is Britain's largest cathedral, appearing to float above the medieval capital city of Yorkshire. Alas, in 1984, it was struck by lightning and nearly burned to the ground. Artisans had a monumental task restoring the 8000 pieces of 12th century stained glass that had fractured into 50,000 fragments.

Tintern Abbey in Gwent, Wales, was fittingly eulogised by Wordsworth for its extraordinary beauty. Built by Cistercian monks in 1131, it is still the most complete of ruined British monasteries.

Scotland is known more for its castles than chuches, but Glasgow Cathedral is the only medieval building not destroyed during the carnage of the Reformation. It dates from the 12th century and houses the tomb of Glasgow's patron, St Mungo.

East Anglia comprises the four counties of Suffolk, Norfolk, Cambridgeshire and Essex with Cambridge being its best-known ecclesiastical and academic attraction. It was founded in the 12th century by Franciscans, Dominicans and Carmelites but it is Ely Cathedral with its unique lantern that stands out. This feat of engineering, a huge octagon of wood and glass, reflects the rays of the dying sun with awesome magnificence.

Norwich has more churches than you care to count – 32 medieval ones within its ancient city walls – and Norwich Cathedral remains one of the most handsome examples of Saxon architecture. Stone for it was quarried in Normandy, France, and brought up river so its spire could rival that of Salisbury.

ART

One of the greatest pleasures of life in Britain is the wealth of art available (largely free) to the public. And it's not just great masterpieces in galleries and museums – art is everywhere in a civilisation that goes back more than a thousand years. The heritage remains in gloriously preserved state or in crumbling relics.

Though not in the same league as the Renaissance cities of Europe, Britain and its artistic heritage speak of a magnificent past full of heraldry and pomp. For art is not merely on tangible canvas but in the splendid auras created by great builders of cathedrals, churches and edifices of historical import. By artisans who created beauty and form in furniture, fabric and works of art.

Britain is seemingly stuffed with great houses and castles which in turn are stuffed with great works of art, furniture and the paraphernalia of grander than grand lifestyles. You could explore a new place everyday for a lifetime. In Scotland alone there are more than 4000 castles. In every village, town, borough or city you will find art in endearing or pretentious forms. A village teashop might display a tapestry from the 17th century. That beautiful chair you sit on in a country pub might have come from a medieval castle. Art is not always in obvious forms. The art of the 15th century blacksmith would be manifest in the fine lines of a portcullis now adorning a country pub.

Galleries and museums are too numerous to name for there are literally thousands of them all over the country. Seek out art through architecture, in the glorious gothic temples to Christianity, Norman churches and Christopher Wren's magnificent domes and turrets.

Stately homes themselves are works of art for such great designs are a thing of the past. Beautiful mouldings, plaster work and sculpture adorn the noble homes now entrusted to the state for upkeep as few private individuals would have the means to do so.

Of those still living in the grand style, the prospect of having tourists gawk at one's private quarters is a heavy, but necessary, price to pay. How else could one raise £1 million a year to maintain 100 rooms, priceless furniture and masterpieces?

A few pounds is a cheap price to pay for the privilege of enjoying such great art by Tintoretto, Rembrandt, Constable, Dali and other great artists. These are the private collections of great families. Others can be seen for free, for example in London's Tate, National and Portrait galleries.

Whichever period, field or style of art you prefer, much abounds in this country for you to enjoy. Half an hour in front of a luscious Vermeer or two hours fathoming Dali's surrealistic genius – they're all available for the price of an ice cream cone, if at all.

Don't pass over the street artists who will paint your portrait for £10, as commercial trash. They are very talented and may be tomorrow's grand masters.

Exhibitions are mounted every so often ranging from mildly pornographic photographs to Indian jewellery. Even department stores cash in on art as a promotional teaser and entire stores often run thematic displays of ethnic or European art forms. Be it in fabric design, furniture or porcelain, the artistic image is irresistible.

In Antiquity

When the Romans left Britain in the early 5th century, the country was plunged into the Dark Ages. However, archaeological finds indicate that the British enjoyed a high level of artistic sophistication even within their barbaric lifestyle. Abstract and symbolic examples of pagan art have been found in ancient buckles and clasps made of gold, glass and enamel from a 7th century ship burial at Sutton Hoo in Suffolk.

By the 11th century, a renaissance of art had come about after Christianity had banished much of the paganism.

After the Norman conquest of 1066, Anglo-Saxon art was greatly influenced by France. The conquerors brought with them a Romanesque style now evident in the awesome carved Apostles of Malmesbury Abbey in Wiltshire and in the 12th century reliefs of Chichester Cathedral.

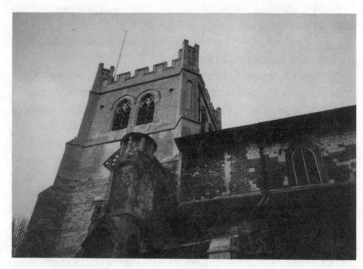

The Norman influence can be seen in medieval art and architecture. Some Norman churches are still in good repair.

By the Middle Ages, the lifestyles of the nobility and Church began to influence art. Sumptuous cloths, devotional ivories and manuscripts were produced for the great courts of Europe but almost exclusively to the glory of God.

The concept of individual artistic genius only emerged at the end of the 16th century, much influenced by the European Renaissance that began in the 14th century in Italy. The best known artist of this Tudor period was the Swiss-German artist Hans Holbein who devoted much of his skills to painting the flamboyant Henry VIII. Some of his best works are in London's National Gallery.

When the Stuart period came, British art flourished. Charles I brought over the talented Flemish Van Dyck, commissioned paintings from Rubens and the first Italianate buildings in England. The Banqueting Hall in Whitehall, London, designed by Inigo Jones, was to affect the whole course of English architecture.

The Restoration period was a time of prosperity, peace and the flourishing of art culminating in the establishment of the Royal Academy in 1768 with the aim of raising artistic status. Among its founder members were some of the greatest names of the world of art – Hogarth, Reynolds, Constable, Gainsborough and Chippendale who put his name and signature on some of the most magnificent examples of English furniture.

By the late 18th century, the penchant for ornate rococo and Chinoiserie began to pale giving way to the 'neo-classicism' much advocated by the Scottish painter and architect, Robert Adam. This was also the period Josiah Wedgwood raised ceramics to a prestigious status. Today, Wedgwood has become a household name in elegance – a much sought-after collectible that graces homes around the world. You can't mistake the characteristic blue or green alabaster with white relief of classical figures on anything from amphorae to ash trays.

With Queen Victoria's ascension to the throne in 1837, artists were freed of the tyranny of portraiture. In its place, piety, patriot-

71

ism and melodrama were dominant moods with a strong strain of the sentimental.

Victorian artefacts became increasingly industrialised, reaching their apogee in the 1851 Great Exhibition at London's Crystal Palace. It was a proclamation to the world of the beauty and eclecticism of Victorian art, many examples of which are still to be found in former colonies.

There was sharp reaction to this mechanisation mania; a nostalgic yearning for the lost paradise of individual craftsmanship. The greatest protagonist was William Morris whose designs have undergone a tremendous rebirth in the last century. His stunning work today adorns homes all over the world, on wallpaper, fabrics and other household accessories. Unfortunately, he could not stem the tide of inevitable marriage between design and machinery which came about in the 20th century.

In Britain and all over the world, visual arts were characterised by extremes and upheavals. The catchwords were abstraction, impressionism, cubism and all other -isms of a period of great artistic ferment. French Surrealists had their English counterparts; Francis Bacon, one of the leading names in figurative painting, distorted reality to express his view of humanity. His works in London's Tate Gallery are startling visages of contortionist nightmare. Henry Moore, born in 1898, overwhelmed the art world with his monumental sculptures. In turn he influenced his students to exploit the texture and colour of steel plates, beams, girders and industrial techniques of welding and riveting.

Post-war Britain saw the need to boost morale and artists of all kinds combined to present an optimism of the nation in the Festival of Britain in 1951. Bacon was still producing sinister art, Moore's protégé Anthony Caro perpetuated his master's massive forms and other 'pop' artists began to come out of the woodwork. Richard Hamilton exploited mass media for his imagery and David Hockney represented a more traditional form of figurative painting.

Surrounded by so much beauty in art, you begin to understand the British loathing for contemporary structures of glass and steel. You begin to appreciate too the value attached to homes with historical character and ambience – as much to preserve their intrinsic value as the perpetuating of craftsmanship that is constantly being threatened by an avalanche of soulless high-tech materials.

As for the street artists mentioned, you'll find them usually near certain art galleries. On weekends in London, practically the entire Bayswater Road becomes a street gallery with paintings and other artistic endeavours hanging on the railings of Hyde Park.

There are too many art schools to mention and where you enrol depends on the field you want to specialise in. Contact your Local Education Authority for information. Better known art schools in London are St Martins which also offers all forms of commercial art and Chelsea Art School. All galleries and museums have an information section which will give you general or specific information about the world of art.

Of the Pop Genre

From posters to hoardings, from body-daubing to surreal sculpture, much that is quintessentially British art takes wild and wacky forms. No idea is too way out to receive public appreciation and artists fairly wallow in a liberalism that allows total expression. Whether it's sketching the glories of a British autumn or indulging in the caricaturing of celebrities, artistic bent is never short of conducive ambience and willing subjects. The entertainment section of most newspapers lists the daily events and exhibitions of the art world.

Chapter Five

THE HOUSE OF WINDSOR

Much as Britain considers itself a modern democratic state, preoccupation and unreserved affection for the monarchy is still very strong. The general feeling is that the royal family should remain detached, aloof even, and keep the certain mysticism that is intrinsic to being royal. Somehow the glamour is tarnished if one of them is seen doing things normal people do – like shopping in a supermarket or swearing. But such is the abiding love of the British people for the royals that scarcely a day passes without the papers coming up with some story or other about the royal goings-on.

Given that the attraction of British royalty brings in unaccountable tourist income, Prince Philip's rather wry remark that "We are not a family but a firm" is understandable. Every single day, rain, shine, sleet or snow, the gates at Buckingham Palace are thick with tourists hoping to catch a glimpse of the most famous personage in the country. Or any lesser royal. Or even the Queen's beloved pet dogs. British royalty live a charmed life as their popularity has hardly waned over the past decades, despite the occasional outcry that 'they're nothing but spongers' living off the public purse.

Despite stories about royal spending habits, size of privy purse and allowances that seem unreal in a world of increasing inflation, the public still regard them with warm fascination. Public criticism and other mud-slinging is met with dignified indifference by royal spokesmen. A rather haughty stand, but the Palace considers comment as beneath their dignity.

The winds of change are about though, especially with younger royals like Prince Charles and his siblings Anne, Andrew and Edward. The Queen herself never grants interviews but it must be a sign of the times when an heir to the British throne works as a tea-boy in a West End theatre! Prince Edward has since moved out to start his own theatre company – still seen as decidedly unroyal.

Prince Edward's decision to leave the royal marines for a life on the boards – albeit behind the scenes – did not meet with his father's approval. It is common knowledge that Prince Philip wants nothing more than that his sons be macho. It is his bad luck that the only child to grow up gutsy and domineering is his only daughter, Princess Anne.

She, the Princess Royal, made front-page news as the result of her separation from her husband, Captain Mark Philips. The tabloids had a field day speculating about the cause of the break-up, but royalty maintained a stiff upper lip. In fact, the princess was in South America when the Palace issued the terse statement that the couple were to separate with no impending divorce. Captain Philips has since moved to a house two miles (3.2 kilometres) from Gatcombe Park where Anne lives with her two children Zara and Peter.

Perhaps mindful of murmurings that they are being distant and out of touch with the common people, the royal children have been very visible and audible over television, giving their views on everything from the environment to union strangleholds. Carefully, royalty avoids involvement with politics and rumour has it that despite their weekly meetings, the Queen and former prime minister Margaret Thatcher could not stand each other's guts.

Royal Ancestry

Largely the British regard their monarchy as a useful institution, a symbol of national identity by its ancient roots and apolitical stance. The Queen can trace her ancestry to the first King of England, Egbert of Wessex in AD 829.

She is also Queen of Scotland and this lineage goes back to Kenneth MacAlpin who established the Kingdom of Scotland in AD 839. Though British monarchy is not the oldest in Europe, it is certainly the most continuous with only an 11-year break between 1649 and 1660. This was when the infamous Oliver Cromwell and his roundheads chopped off the head of King Charles I and the Puritans ruled briefly.

A Darned Good Show

Whatever the reasons for British royalty's endurance and endearance, it's the showbiz side that has the crowds cheering for more. 'A darned good show' as American tourists put it. The pomp and pageantry are very much a public relations exercise.

So are the social activities of the young royals whose every action is minutely reported in the daily tabloid press. This is the side of royalty that visitors first encounter, whether or not they actually get to see Prince Edward brewing tea for Andrew Lloyd Webber!

Why do Prince Charles and Princess Diana have separate bedrooms? They just do, like most upper class couples do, as the media hasten to explain. Why did Mark Philips resolutely refuse to have an

earldom bestowed upon him thus making his children commoners, much to the Queen's annoyance? Perhaps the marriage was already in trouble long before they agreed to separate. Why does Fergie look so frumpy despite spending thousands on her wardrobe? Do they really need a £4 million house? Who was that young man seen on the island of Mustique with Princess Margaret? These and a hundred other posers sell the tabloids and magazines by the millions everyday. There are even magazines devoted exclusively to the goings-on of the royal family – down to the obscure princelings and assorted dukes and earls.

From the inside of the Palace, minor royals have been heard to moan that it's a pain being a blue blood. They have little privacy in public and every minor gaffe, social slip or plain youthful high jinks is chronicled, often blown out of proportion in the press. A picture of Princess Di's bra strap showing caused public furore and the subsequent apology of the newspaper for being trivial. Readers' letters poured in, most with the same complaint that there are more important issues than the royal slip, and designer label or not, it did not merit a front page story. When Prince Charles made a flip remark that he talks to his plants, the press made him out to be something of a nut case. He was certainly not amused but resigned to the fact that every little twitch he makes is going to cause waves.

Princess Anne has been called horsey, bossy and a bitch. Now the feisty lady has redeemed herself by working tirelessly for her Save the Chidren charity, travelling thousands of miles around the world raising money for the underprivileged children. Even with her marriage about to collapse, she was thousands of miles away in Central America. And on television – an act that would have been unthinkable a decade ago – she excelled herself by answering questions from the audience with a disarming, self-effacing wit that won her even more fans.

And when Princess Di holds the hands of an AIDS child sufferer, the public just about sanctifies her. To her credit, the gauche Diana Spencer has transformed herself from a pudgy upper class girl into Britain's favourite cover girl. She even took the stage one evening as a surprise for her husband. Dancer Wayne Sleep, all of five feet (1.5 metres), tossed the nearly six foot (1.8 metres) Princess in a sexy *pas-de-deux*. Royalists dropped their pince nez in horror at the antics of their future queen. This little jest did not harm her public image one jot though traditionalists were aghast that their future queen should have given such a vulgar display.

I found myself being more absorbed each day with every new story about the British royals, as you no doubt will. The media certainly know how to package them and they sell like no other. Every time Princess Di appears on a magazine cover, it breaks all circulation records. It seems her only rival in the popularity stakes is the Queen Mother, affectionately called Queen Mum. This grand old lady who recently turned 90 can do no wrong in the eyes of the press and her adoring public. All floaty chiffons and pastel silks, she still puts in a respectable workload of appearances annually. And her birthday has become a national affair.

Royal workload is another favourite dartboard for the anti-royal public. Who wouldn't enjoy cutting ribbons and opening horse shows for £100,000 a year? And so it goes on.

Royal Quirks

Whether you care a hoot or not, royal behaviour makes interesting, and often mildly shocking, reading. Some of the trivia that sneaked out of the Palace:

- The Queen feeds her corgis herself with fillet of beef from a silver salver and with a silver fork. A royal 'pooper scooper' attendant takes care of the afters with a different sort of salver and gets paid to do the job full time!
- The Queen Mum has two alabaster angels beside her bed and insists on a daily change of their robes.
- The Queen travels with her own toilet seat and feather pillows. She is the only person in Britain who travels without a passport. And the only person for whom Harrods used to close its doors to the public for one day a year so she could do her Christmas shopping. But she doesn't carry money even though bank notes have her picture on them.
- Princess Margaret leases her island home on Mustique when she's not there and is so mean she won't patch a hole in the washbasin. A Sunday magazine showed the royal crack in full colour.

The public, it seems, cannot get enough of such nuggets of information and, no doubt, as a first time visitor, you will be just as enchanted. It's no different from reading about the stardust and glitz of Hollywood. Which also explains why many Americans are besotted with both. Because they haven't got royalty and film stars come closest in the throned firmament.

Anti-Royalists

In truth, the band of fierce anti-royalists is small even among a large republican mass. At worst royalty is thought of as being irrelevant and a waste of public taxes. Some grudgingly concede that much tourism revenue would be lost without the royal show. The irritant seems to be the privy purse paid out of public funds. What, for example, does Princess Margaret do each year to earn hundreds of thousands of pounds? The Queen's allowance runs into millions but most of it goes into maintaining the royal lifestyle – which brings the argument back to tourist revenue. Just how much of state and private money is spent maintaining the royal status of an ever-growing family is a fact that the media are not prepared to explore to the full. At the time of going to print, the Queen is paying taxes for the first time in her long reign.

By and large, public murmurings are just that. The press may occasionally question the justification of the Duchess of York taking six months out of a year for holidays while being paid for it. But as the Palace never comments on press stories, ambivalent public feelings simply dissipate.

Several times a year, the Queen holds garden parties as a gesture towards meeting her public in an informal setting. If you were one of the lucky thousands to get invited, you would have been vetted very carefully. You would have done something worthy, in the world of business, sport, entertainment or simply a noble deed worthy of public recognition.

Royal Riches

The Queen is deemed to be one of the richest women in the world, if not the richest. But it is highly unlikely that she could ever liquidate her priceless paintings, jewellery and property and hop it to live in grand style on some private island. Most of the royal abodes and property they're on belong to the state and the Queen actually owns only Sandringham in Norfolk and Balmoral Castle in Scotland.

She may own priceless crowns and jewels but they're a part of the monarchical repository and she could no more sell the sceptre than President Bush can the White House. For all being surrounded by galleries stuffed with priceless masterpieces, the Queen remains a country woman at heart and is happiest walking her dogs and mucking about in the heather on long walks.

Prince Charles has been known to criticise the amount Princess Diana spends on her wardrobe. In her defence, Princess Di almost always wears clothes by British designers, thereby waving the flag for the British fashion industry. No sooner is she seen sporting some fashion than the high street stores are scrambling to sell copies. As public relations go, she is seen as a solid gold for the industry.

Fergie, the Duchess of York, has been criticised for her tacky attempt to earn revenue from writing children's books. If the newspaper stories are to be believed, first she promised to donate the money to charity and then pocketed most of the half million pounds or so in royalties in her own pocket. She was alleged to have accepted a large sum from a tabloid for publishing interviews with her. All this has led to some public censure and it is whispered among royal gossip grapevines that the Queen has had to pull her aside for a few words of advice about royal dignity.

Whatever their foibles, the fairy-tale existence of some and the common touch of others, British royalty is an integral part of British life. Love 'em or hate 'em, they're here to stay and more likely to carry on for the next 1000 years.

Chapter Six

THE BRITISH WAY OF LIFE

DYED-IN-THE-WOOL HABITS

The British are, by and large, creatures of rather fixed habits. The following must be viewed in general light and not as a statistical study. It is not possible to pigeonhole individuals and cite specific numbers. Attitudes are changing all the time, but it is my personal observation – and that of many Brits I have met – that this conservatism is more the norm than the exception.

A little old lady will dine on the same day each week, at the same table in the same restaurant of the same dish for years and think it perfectly normal. Psychologists say it's a fear of the unknown, especially for old people who lived through the hardship of the Second World War. The very familiarity of steak and kidney pie every Wednesday serves to calm an old person's fears by its very predictability. Others, even the younger set, are wont to eat three times a week at the same restaurant, more or less at the same time and preferably at the same table and off the same menu! Conservative? Yet he may be eating something quite exotic for an Englishman. Lasagne is exotic for an Englishman, a dyed-in-the-wool chap not given to impulse.

Suggest to an Englishman to do something quite mad like walking down Oxford Street in his pyjamas and he will probably have a fit. Yet, paradoxically, Britain has produced the most idiosyncratic people, the most adventurous. The first to scale Mount Everest, the first to dive under the South Pole or some other derring do. After all, when Great Britain ruled the waves, the British were everywhere from wildest Africa to Boston.

Most old age pensioners live out the rest of their lives in a well-ordered manner because their incomes do not stretch to rash, impulsive spending. Yet, it is not the thought of spending more money than they can afford but doing something out of the ordinary that they baulk at. Every Saturday night at the same pub, drinking the same amount of the same brew seems to be comforting assurance.

People will spend their holidays in the same places at the same time each year – quite often traditional holiday camps like Butlin's or Pontin's where everything is run on the same well-ordered lines. Assembly line activities and food are grist to the Englishman's leisure mill. Recently a retired couple were given a special treat by the hotel they had been staying in for the last 30 years every year at the same time!

Going up a notch or two, the Briton will holiday in the same European country, usually Spain, year in year out. The thought of anything more foreign than that is distinctly unappealing. It also helps to understand why the Spanish authorities bend over backwards to provide the comforting sustenance of typical British food in Majorca, Costa del Sol or wherever the millions of British spend their holidays. The number of British who venture further afield are a pin drop compared to the masses who make their annual exodus to well-tried and tested spots.

It took me a while to cotton on to why on certain days, backyards are awash with drying laundry. The routine of a particular day for doing laundry best exemplifies this entrenched sense of regularity. It matters little that it's pouring with rain on that day. Wash day is wash day and not even the foulest of inclement weather can nudge the ritual among many. The clothes simply dry indoors.

To be fair this is only typical of the average family with working husband, housebound wife and small children. There is diffusion when it comes to single people and those living a more peripatetic lifestyle. Even so, some will faithfully drag their dirty laundry on a given day each week to the laundromat.

Manufacturers of household goods, via their advertising agencies, thrive on this predictability and are reticent to change their creative platforms. Perhaps the most visible adherence to unchanging habits is in the royal family's lifestyle. The Queen has not changed her hairstyle since the 50s and magazines defend that her tiara can only sit on such coiffure. Nor did she change her couturier for decades until her favourite Norman Hartnell died. Then she opted for someone just as traditional, Hardy Amies. As a result, her dress preference still reflects a time two decades past.

Prince Charles was coaxed out of his boring grey suits by his more hip wife but he still sticks to his ageless garb. More significant is the fact that he has never been seen in jeans. Princess Anne is known to live to eat and will happily dine on smoked salmon every day of the year unless when she is travelling. Perhaps they are privileged in being able to indulge thus, but it serves to illustrate the British penchant for familiarity and the comfort therein.

In every sphere of live, this slowness and reluctance to adapt to change has been detrimental to the smooth running of public organisations. Changes to the transport system, be it newfangled turnstiles in the Underground or a new colour for telephone boxes, usually meet with some resistance. Or even vehement outcry. When British Telecom began switching their traditional red phone boxes for more high-tech yellow, green and gun metal ones, you could have heard the public howl of protest clear across the country. Rich Americans have been known to buy these red phone boxes to be converted into shower stalls!

The argument that history is being compromised for technology – usually regarded as dubious at best and downright sacrilegious at worst – is spat out with great vehemence. The technocrats are usually unmoved and the authorities invariably go the way of progress. Lobbying for reversal can become quite fierce and for every defender of the high-tech, there are dozens of protestors against unfeeling change.

A sympathetic observer might see it all as a concerted effort to preserve Nature's handiwork. But with relevance to progress and development, such outcry often seems out of proportion to the importance of the defended object. Prince Charles has even published a book with critical observation of what architects have done to the British landscape. His description of a high-rise block minces no words. He wants all development to be along the lines of historical buildings and at the moment he isn't thought of too kindly by most forward looking architects. Again, it's the thought of change that both frightens and bewilders him. The argument against him in its most valid form is that he has little knowledge of what it might cost to engage artisans for all those curlicues and sculpture he thinks all buildings should have. But this is simply one example of an entrenched attitude against change that has received media blowout because of who he is. The commoner too is often heard to bemoan that modern houses are nothing more than little boxes. But a box with minarets, turrets, gargoyles or even a modest portico will drive housing prices even higher than they already are. And he would be the first person to object to this if he is in the market for a house.

If you decide to have an impromptu party and invite friends over at short notice – like one day – don't expect any sort of turnout. For one thing the British plan things way ahead and chances are your friends would have fixed up their social calendar weeks, if not months, in advance. Even if they are not otherwise occupied, doing social things on impulse is basically against their nature. It's inexplicable but that's the way most British are – something I had to get used to after frustrating attempts to coral people at last minute's notice. This explains why many things have remained the same for hundreds of years. It took me months before I could find a stove wide enough to accommodate a Chinese *wok* and a pot at the same time. Then again it was Italian.

INSTITUTIONS

Not, as you might think, great edifices of academe but reference to the dyed-in-the-wool things that reflect the very soul of Britishness. Without the need for a single word or protracted prose, these give the British their sense of identity and uniqueness. Some have been embraced by commercialism and traded in for profit, perhaps all to the good, and often thrust upon the world as 'touristy collectibles'. The pragmatic will say it can only mean immortality but others deplore the consumer-orientated fate of their beloved icons. Many have been miniaturised into tourist kitsch.

Just what these are, a foreigner may not know immediately but will begin to understand in time why some things never change in this country. For many conservatives, these are the very things that give them the emotional security in a world that seems bent on spinning itself into the frightening sphere of mass production and homogeneous multiplicity.

Burberry Raincoat

As British as Big Ben and for which hordes of Japanese tourists gladly fork out hundreds of pounds. What set out to be a practical wet weather garment has now been elevated to the hall of fame, not quite in the same way as the kimono is to the Japanese, but nearly there. In a style that has remained unchanged for decades, beige with check interfacing, wearing one reflects not mere fashion but the epitome of Britishness. By a stroke of economic necessity, Burberry's has been sold to a Japanese conglomerate.

Wellington Boots

Who would think a pair of humble black, or the more upmarket green rubber boots for tramping around the garden would become an institution? Yet, they are, for a few pounds, as British as can be. Named after the Duke of Wellington, Wellies, as they are called, are essential to the true Briton to venture into his garden in slushy weather. The Duke would turn in his grave to see the many versions of his Wellie – from porcelain vases to money boxes.

Paddington Bear

A cuddly toy, nay, much more for it always wears a classic duffle coat that is the uniform cover for millions of British school kids. A character much loved by young and old.

Earl Grey Tea

Not just any tea, Earl Grey marks a gentleman and reflects an elegant tradition. Earl Grey tea in fine bone china – who needs coffee?

Tartan

Really Scottish of bold checks, each design is the symbol of this clan or that. Tartan pure wool scarves, skirts and kilts have remained untouched by the flights of fashion for centuries.

Three-Piece Pinstripe Suit

Defiant of the capricious nature of men's fashions, a three-piece pinstripe suit has been distinguishing the English city gentry from any other for decades.

Oxford Brogues

Stout shoes of the English country squire genre that no true Brit would be without.

Tweed

This spawned the 'tweedy set': conservative and countrified. It is usually worn by people of refinement. A true classic in any wardrobe, it has remained untouched by the changing trends of fashion.

London Taxis

These deceivingly lumberous black cabs, though typical of London, have come to be an internationally recognised symbol of Britain for their stolid dependability and comfort.

The Ritz Hotel

In London's Piccadilly, it spawned the very epitome of style – hence the word 'ritzy', meaning everything classy.

Travel in comfort in the London taxi; spacious, it gives you a lot of leg room and allows you to bring big pieces of luggage on board.

Wedgwood

Which visitor has not succumbed to buying something of Josiah Wedgwood's? The classic blue or green alabaster china in myriad forms of ornamental or functional use is so distinctive you cannot miss them.

Fish and Chips

Wrapped in newspaper, generally a tabloid, fish and chips are still the lifeblood of hungry Britons seeking cheap, familiar and beloved sustenance. As a general rule, the further north you travel, the better they are.

Sausages

Fat, pork or beef sausages are the very soul of a British breakfast, cooked and served a million times across the country each day.

Roast Beef and Yorkshire Pudding

If English (the Scottish and Welsh set much less store on this

The Great British Invention: with a liberal sprinkling of vinegar, fish and chips wrapped in newspaper makes a delicious meal for thousands of people.

89

national dish) cuisine has a representative, this is it. If you cannot make a decent roast beef and Yorkshire pudding, you might as well not be English.

Punch

This magazine takes a look at British life with a wickedness that belies belief. As British as any other symbol though magazines come and magazines go. *Private Eye*, a fortnightly satirical magazine, goes considerably further with muck-raking probes into the lives of political, entertainment and financial high-fliers. Forever being sued for libel, the magazine has an immense following and its city analysis and comments are followed closely by all involved in the financial sector, since there's usually more truth than fiction.

Measurements

Although Britain has been metric for over a decade, and its EC partners all operate on a metric system, the old imperial system is strangely persistent. You will thus notice all supermarket and grocery produce has both metric and imperial quantities – as do all cookery books. While a few modern thinking boroughs begin to implement local footpath notices with distances in kilometres, all road signs are still in miles – as are all published maps. No amount of legislation will prevent the British from drinking a pint of beer or the daily milkman from delivering his pints of milk.

Children in school are taught to measure in metric millimetres and centimetres, fabric is sold in metric lengths, but planks and widths of wood remain in inches.

FOOD

On the whole, British food, as you would find it in the motorway service stations, pubs, cafes and chain restaurants along every high street, runs the gamut between mildly interesting and plain boring. Meat, poultry, fish, peas, carrots and chips are the order of the day unless you have a budget that stretches to more upmarket establishments. Then again the only difference might be the plate in which your carrots and peas come. Since there are relatively few restaurants offering traditional dyed-in-the-wool British fare – when the British eat out, they prefer continental – you have to contend with the aforementioned fast fare.

British food, be it Scottish haggis, Welsh rarebit or English stew, is alive and well only if you seek it hard and far afield enough. You will also find the British rather apologetic about their food. It will take you a while to understand that not everyone is passionate about food, the British among the very least. Drink, yes.

Oriental and continental cuisines have far more to offer in terms of savoury choices and even a fast-food pizza is still more palatable

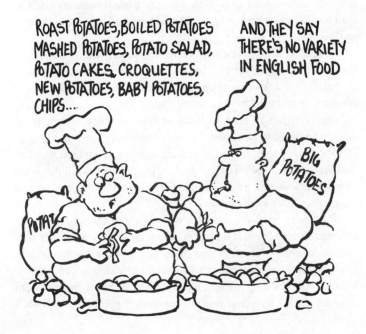

ROAST POTATOES, BOILED POTATOES MASHED POTATOES, POTATO SALAD, POTATO CAKES, CROQUETTES, NEW POTATOES, BABY POTATOES, CHIPS....

AND THEY SAY THERE'S NO VARIETY IN ENGLISH FOOD

BIG POTATOES

than a dry cold Bacon Lettuce and Tomato (BLT) sandwich. If you are not too picky, there are a number of places in every town, city and usually along the high street that sell one or the other of the American or continental fast food products.

Supermarkets can be a tasty answer to the lack of ethnic dishes. Most outlets (and there are thousands in Britain under the Marks & Spencer, Sainsbury, Safeway and Tesco banners – the major chains) now stock a basic range of Chinese, Indian, continental and some Southeast Asian products. The rest is up to your cooking skills and ingenuity. In addition, supermarkets are stocking more and more ready-to-eat dishes, especially Italian, Indian and Chinese, even a few Thai and Indonesian ones. The Japanese supermarket chain Yaohan recently opened its first ever supermarket and shopping mall in Europe, in Colindale, Northwest London and offers a wide range of fresh sushi fish as well as ready-packed sushi meals. The mall also boasts several ethnic restaurants including a sushi counter and noodle shop.

Generally, all over Britain, there is a supermarket near where you live that stocks enough basics for anyone to whip up home-cooked fare at a fraction of the cost of eating out. £35 will get four people a very basic meal in a restaurant. The same amount buys enough groceries to feed a family of four for three to four days. Also, what used to be esoteric is now commonly available as long as your tastes do not extend to gourmet rarities. Even then, you can find these in the London area – shark's fin, ginseng, caviar that costs as much as a week's wages for one silver-forkful, whatever – if you are prepared to pay the price.

Short-term residents and students will either have limited or no facilities to cook, even if they do have some culinary skills. For flat-sharers, the discovery of a British kitchen is short-lived euphoria. Even if you stay long enough to warrant stocking up on utensils basic to your cooking. Most are poky with just about enough room to swing a cat. Or the equipment is so basic that eating out seems a better option. Longer-term residents, less concerned about finding a cheap inner city bedsit, will find that British houses and even large apartments do have large enough kitchens. Many British families indeed would have a dining table to eat most meals in the kitchen.

Be adventurous and make forays into the local food scene much as even the British themselves admit to a bland, stodgy cuisine. There is good English food, not necessarily of the savoury genre, to be found in some places. Traditional cream tea for instance, with hot scones, home-made jam and thick clotted cream is as British as can be. Enjoy it for its intrinsic worth even if you suspect the jam comes from a supermarket bottle.

More upmarket places like the Beefeater chain do excellent roasts if you are a serious meat eater. When you're miles from anywhere, diving into the first ethnic takeaway can be more of a shock than a good meal of roast meat, potatoes and two vegetables.

With the advent of chain merchandising on the premise of value for money and catering to the conservative masses, the food scene invariably suffers. Throughout the British Isles, you will come upon eateries like Little Chef and the Happy Eater among others, located at just the place when your hunger pains begin to gnaw and there's nothing else for miles around.

With such a captive market, they don't need to apologise for being the antithesis of cordon bleu cookery. But then they are catering for Joe Public who is more used to potatoes and meat. You might have to psyche yourself before breaking journey for a meal at one of these places. And when the waitress microwaves your Danish pastry till it sticks to the plate, you feel like biting yourself.

Tired salads, dry burgers, microwaved-to-death pastries nonetheless are better than nothing when you're 100 miles (162 kilometres) from the nearest hot dog kiosk. Unless you opt for safe American or Italian fast food. No shocks here but they are much more widespread in the provincial towns than in the big cities that have a clutch – at least a few – of ethnic eateries.

The shock comes when you go a little more upmarket to French cuisine. A simple meal of soup, main meat course and a sweet can set you back £25 per head or more at a restaurant proper. The lovely ambience you pay for. They cater mainly to local residents who like an occasional night out replete with silver service, supercilious waiters and pricy wines. Curiously, much as the British say they hate the French, dining out Gallic style is very much a social priority. It gives them the chance to show off a nouveau oenophilist knowledge, bury their own meat and two veg for a while and generally soak up the elegance of being treated like sophisticated gourmets. Of course restaurateurs riding on these pretensions charge a premium for their European culinary refinement.

Pub Food
Pub food is good value and easily available. As well as the tradi-

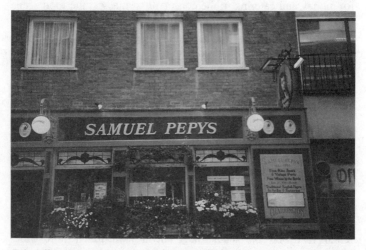

Pubs offer cheap and hearty food, a variety of beers and ales, and a great atmosphere. Literature is not left out either, as shown by this pub sporting the name of famous 18th century diarist Samuel Pepys.

tional ploughman's lunch of bread, cheese, cold meat and pickles, many pubs – particularly those in the countryside – offer a range of hot dishes as well as salads and desserts. It is well worth purchasing a guide to good pubs and their food if you are touring the country, as a visit to a pleasant pub, serving well-kept real ale and a hearty meal, can really be a highpoint of your sightseeing. Do be careful not to expect too much at all pubs: traditionally they are drinking places, and many still keep to this role. Others will stop serving lunch at 2 p.m. sharp on Sundays and may not serve any food on Sunday evenings.

You are allowed to take children into a pub to eat food with the landlord's permission: they should obviously not consume alcohol. Again, up-to-date guides to British pubs will list those which are children-friendly and those where you can be assured of peace from children's screams.

The British Cafe

Were it not for the proliferation of American-style fast food joints, this British tradition would still hold sway among those who can find joy in sausages, eggs, chips, baked beans and toast. Born of the transport workers' need for cheap, hearty fare, and later spreading to the high street corner, cafes (pronounced 'caff') are distinguishable for being unprepossessing, with formica-topped tables, the ubiquitous bottle of HP sauce, cheerful service and cheap prices. It is a tradition that is being threatened by the equally cheap but lickety-split service of the hamburger, pizza or fried chicken genre.

Home-Cooked Food

When invited to a British home for a meal, expect simple fare, usually meticulously or elegantly served. The British are not into buffets or an elaborate menu when entertaining. A typical meal for most on weekends – the only time real cooking is done– is a roast, masses of potatoes and a vegetable or two, usually peas and carrots.

There is also a growing trend among many upwardly mobile people to buy ready-to-heat stuff from the supermarkets, so expect a meal to be a mish-mash of pasta, *sushi* and sweet-and-sour Tesco this or Sainsbury that.

Feasts Not So Unlimited

You'd be lucky to get more than cold meat and salad at a British function, and many British 'drinks parties' or 'cocktail parties' are precisely that, with perhaps peanuts or other nibbles to help wash down whatever you are drinking. In fact, food is low priority at most functions apart from private dinner parties when perhaps a particular host is a foodie and you can get an interesting meal. Or it came from professional caterers who can make a salmon look like a Rembrandt still life.

Otherwise the standard fare is soup, meat, salad, pies, chips and bread. You get much the same at English restaurants but served with panache, and at a price.

There is however a lot of media coverage of good British food that the Victorians enjoyed. When this will translate into commercially available repasts is hard to say. But if you try cooking them at home, it might at least be therapeutic enough to diffuse the shock of missing the familiar.

Trad British Food

Sadly, traditional British food, like the mashed pie and eel, is rare and getting rarer. Even that seaside delight of whelks and assorted crustacea served with vinegar and salt is fast disappearing in the face of the fast food explosion. Such seaside resorts like Brighton (the pier has been beautifully refurbished), Bournemouth, Margate and Blackpool, in fact wherever there is a pier, used to feature this traditional British seafood stall. Today, you have to look hard for it and then the whelks come in plastic tubs.

As for fish and chips wrapped in old copies of *The Times* –

forget it. I have not had one good fish and chip meal in six years and even when sent to the so-called best places in and outside London, always came back with the same dismally tired chips and battered to death skate, cod or halibut.

I once asked a friend to take me to a place known for its eel and mash pie (a Victorian culinary gem). Tongue drooling, we made for the place somewhere in Enfield and found to our horror a large sign advertising the impending opening of yet another pizza place! He was flummoxed as to where else one could go for such historical servings. Such is the influx of American fast food that the best of British has been shell-shocked out of existence. Some things, sadly, the British have not been able to preserve.

Traditional English food is sadly fast disappearing. What is advertised as 'Traditional English Fayre' is alas a far cry from the genuine thing.

97

ETHNIC FOOD

On the whole the food scene in Britain is pretty cosmopolitan outside the posh nosh offered by five star hotels. But then when you convert a £30 per head meal of hot soup, meat and gateau, the shock can send you right back to your kitchen. One really upmarket French place charges £180 per head for soup, fish, meat and dessert!

But be advised that what you read on the menu isn't always what you expect. The interpretation of any foreign food can be far off course. Reconstituted dry rice noodles given two stirs in a *wok* do not a noodle dish make. Nor what passes for spaghetti bolognese, unless it is a reputable Italian establishment. The point is most are geared to what the British are familiar with – not too rich, not too spicy, in other words, anglicised beyond the pale. Some restaurant chefs will do the fine tuning, but it comes with a hefty price tag.

The shocks will dissipate when you learn to cook and buy in bulk where you can find your favourite vegetables and spices. But then you might even get to like British food. Which will send the British into shock. But underlining this, any British will warm to you if you genuinely show your appreciation for their culinary tradition. Which is the whole point about assimilating and alleviating culture shock.

Mexican

Another buzz word in Britain is hot Mexican food. Well, Tex-Mex at least. The sum total of this cuisine is hot *salsa* – a fiery sauce made with chopped tomatoes and chillies. And it goes on everything, from *tortillas* to *enchiladas*. And cheese goes on everything, melted in the oven till it bubbles.

Indian

From the Sub-continent comes the ubiquitous *tandoori* that you can take or leave. North Indian food is now so familiar in Britain that you will find a restaurant in virtually every small town in the South and Midlands. Indian restaurants wisely stay open after pub closing hours, catering for those beer-induced hungers. Some restaurants – you'll soon discover these – have a penchant for preparing every dish in the same sauce and usually swimming in oil. It's a matter of time before you discover the good ones and those best avoided. Happily, with so much competition from the other ethnic establishments, even the most complacent restaurateurs are pulling themselves up by the apron strings. Media food critics can be positively vitriolic when a restaurant they review tries to pull one over.

Chinese

It would come as a great surprise to many British to hear that there are many different types of Chinese food. The most common type in Britain is the high street takeaway restaurant, serving a pseudo Cantonese style of bland flavoured fried rice, sweet-and-sour pork, chicken with cashewnuts and so on. Some Chinese takeaways have even assimilated to British taste so much that they serve fish and chips and mushy peas as well as spring rolls and prawn crackers.

Restaurants in London's Chinatown and elsewhere in bigger cities do serve a wide variety of dishes at a variety of prices and degrees of excellence.

Mediterranean

Greek (actually Cypriot), Lebanese and other Middle Eastern offerings are pretty much basic meat and rice meals without spices. One of the most familiar sights along high streets in towns and cities is the *donner kebab* restaurant. Cheap and plentiful, they are always available when you need to satisfy your hunger pangs, though the quality varies enormously.

Southeast Asian

When the British discovered Southeast Asian food some time in the early 70s, they could not get enough of it. But unless you live in

London, it is still comparatively rare.

However, Southeast Asian restaurants are now slowly opening up in places like Cambridge, Oxford and Brighton. They are not as widespread as traditional Chinese takeaways but are at least on the bandwagon. Many now sell *satay* – or a version of it.

For want of a more precise description, most restaurants serving Southeast Asian food are called Malaysian because, outside the mainland Chinese and Hong Kong community, Malaysians constitute the largest group of Chinese from Asia. Japan is not trailing far behind now, with huge Japanese investments being pumped into the car industry necessitating a large corps of Japanese personnel. And the Japanese will trade their best Datsun for a good *sushi* meal.

A few shopping malls in London (Whiteleys in Bayswater, The Trocadero in the West End and The Plaza on Oxford Street) now offer cooked ethnic food in an open plan.

THE ETHNIC SHOPPER

For everything Chinese, Soho has supermarkets like Loon Fung, Golden Gate, See Woo and Cheong Leen leading the field in merchandise. They stock every conceivable Chinese food and fresh vegetables hitherto unknown in Britain.

For Southeast Asian produce, the Mata Hari chain of supermarkets in Bayswater, Kilburn and Tooting are veritable Thai/Indonesian emporiums with such esoterics as banana leaf, banana bud, lemon grass, etc, available all year round.

In the area of Southall you would think you are walking down a street in Bombay. This Indian enclave screams spices and saris and is a wonderful discovery trip for those enamoured of curries.

RESTAURANTS

Restaurant hours are fairly consistent throughout Britain. Most open at 12 noon until 3 p.m. and again between 7 p.m. and 11 p.m. Touristy towns might have late night hours until midnight or even 1 a.m. Sunday opening is geared mainly to places that attract large numbers of visitors, such as Soho, Stratford-upon-Avon, Windsor, Brighton and other day-tripper centres. Otherwise, most establishments operate a six-day week to avoid running into overtime wages and equipment fatigue.

Service

Wide ranging, from toffee-nosed French-style replete with floor-sweeping aprons and thinly-veiled distaste for unsuitably-dressed customers to rowdy Italian family-type and plain rude Chinese. One restaurant in London's Chinatown has the dubious reputation of being cheap and most uncheerful. Whatever their secret formula for success, it is usually packed day and night.

Whatever you do, don't plonk yourself at the first empty table. It is an unwritten law that you wait to be seated by the waiter or waitress at a table he or she designates. Any vehement choice for a particular table is likely to be met with a cold eye and a sharp tongue. The place might look half-empty but every house has its own system of seating, not to mention a waiter's particular whim.

At places mindful of professional service, you will be given a menu and a wine list for some five minutes to study. At others not so inclined, you might be ignored for 10 minutes before being attended to. Be patient – they're just busy, not indifferent. Expect to wait an average of 10 minutes for your starters to arrive. Restaurants tend to cancel tables if customers turn up more than 45 minutes late.

If you have a predilection for extras, ask for them when the order is being taken. There is no more unpopular customer than one who gesticulates several times for water, ice, sauces ad infinitum. Plain water is never served unless you ask for it. Nothing is for free in this country and most places will ask if you mean mineral or spa water which costs about £1 per glass. You are likely to get withering looks if you ask for six glasses of plain water because there's nothing in it for the waiter.

A restaurant that seats 60 people will have no more than four or five waiting staff, usually rushed off their feet. Excessive demands will only be met by curt reaction or outright insolence. Few restaurants in Britain have a retinue of staff hovering to serve every little whim. For this kind of service at high-class places, expect to pay £30 per head. Top professional service comes with a hefty price tag. It is a known fact that highly-skilled waiting staff earn up to £300 a week – net. More than twice what a schoolteacher earns.

Ethnic restaurants are more laid back in service and, being smaller – average seating 35 people – manage better with one waiter than large establishments with six. Smaller establishments also depend more on tips than those backed by a conglomerate or chain.

Tips

10% is the norm, though a recent law prohibits this from being printed on a bill, and it has to be totally discretionary. But, as an entrenched habit, tipping is a common practice. Waiting staff are not about to have the carpet pulled from under them and generous tips mean less skating on financial thin ice. Say weekly takings are £5000 in a four waiter place. 10% or £500 divided by four means a tax-free £125 on top of the basic £50.

On the other hand, don't tip if service is most unsatisfactory. Or tip more if you have been particularly well-served. Tourists and back-packers are not the most popular customers as they are notorious for not leaving enough tips or any at all. One other good tip: become a waiter to earn extra cash. All you need is common sense, steady hands and sturdy feet. It's also probably the profession with the highest turnover, so there are always jobs a-begging.

Eating Modes

Thankfully, few continental restaurants intimidate with a battery of knives, forks and spoons, even for an elegant meal. The basis is a butter knife, meat and fish knives, a soup spoon and a dessert spoon.

The usual pattern is to work from the outside in, but most establishments now lay cutlery depending on what you order. Since most waiters will pour your first glass of wine, there is less reason for nervousness when dining posh.

Most Asians used to street hawker food find eating on the run – or rather, on the stroll – a natural habit. The British recoil at this simply because they do not have a hawker heritage and are self-conscious about eating in public. Fast food is eaten on the premises and those seen eating outdoors are usually visitors or young people with no such pretention. I know friends who would not even eat a fruit unless they are indoors.

The National Cuppa

The Japanese may have elevated the drinking of tea to an art form. The British regard it with no less reverence, if differently. Next to the weather, tea is probably the most favourite subject of conversation. Nowhere else would you see such passion for a beverage. It is almost a national panacea for all ills and assorted chills; the watery British sun rises and sets on tea – Earl Grey, Lapsang Soochong, Orange Pekoe and whatever else the plantations in faraway India and China may yield.

A true Brit would be loath to greet the day without a steaming 'cuppa', an affectionate colloquialism and the pulse of British life. Everyone drinks a few cups a day. Indeed, 'having a cuppa' is a national advertising tagline on buses, hoardings, television and radio.

It brings a smile to the face of an old age pensioner the way caviar and lobster would not. It uplifts and soothes, whatever the leaf, served in fine bone china or in cracked tin cup.

Real tea-drinkers will swear by age-old rituals. The water must be boiling hot, first to rinse the pot and then to brew the tea. Even though tea merchants have put them in practical bags, purists will insist on brewing their cuppa from loose leaves.

Tea, in short, is not merely a hot beverage to warm oneself. It is as British as the Union Jack, to be indulged in with the utmost sobriety and reverence or jovial bonhomie, in humble homes or grand salons. Even the tea lady, once a ubiquitous feature in offices, has become something of a symbol of endearment.

Today, most tea retailing companies resort to this tradition as unique selling point. One brand goes even further – using a bunch of chimpanzees to caricature the tradition and embracing the jollity of blue-rinsed ladies and salt-of-the-earth British gentlemen chuntering over their brew. Does it sell the stuff? By the millions, even in bags. It is the British wry sense of humour at work and, far from taking offence at being so likened, the public lap it up by the pot.

When invited to a British home, the first thing you're likely to be offered is a cup of tea. When you accept it, it will pull you close to the bosom of the people. Which is what living here is all about.

In factories all over Britain, 'elevenses' are a sacrosanct part of the working day. It means that, come eleven o'clock, everyone, barring the go-getting workaholic, breaks for tea. It may be a can of coke or a sneaked glass of wine, but the reference is always to 'tea break'. Even the looming presence of a coffee machine does not detract from a beloved custom.

Even when organisations like British Rail are lambasted for indifferent food, the key issue is invariably tea. BBC disc-jockeys, in self-effacing mood, make fun of their canteen tea. In one programme the prize for a quiz is, guess what? BBC tea bags. And the obsession goes down the line. Workmen at construction sites all over the country will down tools in unison for a communal pot of the brew. Members of Parliament will put aside matters of state for a 15-minute tea break.

Even if you are not a tea-drinker, you will find yourself drawn to this charming tradition. Coming in from battling the cold wind, a hot cup of tea courses through your system like a gush of warmth.

PUNCTUALITY

It wouldn't be fair to assume a picture of national unease but the British tend to be less bothered about being clockwork punctual than, say, the Swiss. Generally, they dislike rushing and pell-mell activity that characterises faster-living societies. Outside the cities, especially London, people thrive on a much slower-paced lifestyle that not all foreigners fully understand or tolerate at first.

It is not in the British psyche to squeeze 25 hours out of 24, barring the workaholics. As a foreigner, you will encounter this first – from the airport to the railway station to the hotel reception. Why is everyone so slow? But you get used to this. As for lateness in appointments, there are attendant reasons, given the variability of travel and weather conditions. In London especially and other urban

sprawls, public transport schedules and perpetual city centre congestion make mincemeat of appointment times. When someone agrees to meet you at 10 a.m. from perhaps 50 miles (80 kilometres) away, you can expect him to be delayed anywhere between half an hour and two hours. The great ribbon tarmacs criss-crossing Britain are a dream to drive on when nothing untoward happens. It takes but one minor accident to cause a traffic jam and resultant tailback stretching for miles. And once on the motorway, you can do nothing except creep, jerk and crawl until the next junction or roundabout where, with any luck, you might find an alternative route.

Social events tend to be the most affected by unpunctuality. British people are averse to being like clockwork when having fun. It's not rudeness if people turn up later than specified, but simply a laid-back attitude towards leisure pursuits. It's not a matter of life and death to be punctual.

However some people take this to extremes and do not show up at all without any explanation. They are usually service people like plumbers or repairmen. And they always give a plausible reason.

You just have to get used to the largely inexplicable tardiness of repairmen. This is not a national lacklustre attitude, to be fair. There are often extenuating circumstances that, unfortunately, you will not know about until you've torn your hair out by the clump. Traffic jams, delays in previous jobs, etc. They do not treat the customer like he's the be-all and end-all, simply because there's more work than they can cope with. Hence the cost of repairing anything.

Don't forget too that the size of the population means you simply have to wait in line – be it repairing a faulty phone or a washing machine. Few after sales services will commit themselves to a fixed time. At best, it will be a.m. or p.m. At worst, it'll be 'sometime in the week'.

Public transport is much more guilty of tardiness than the individual. All bus stops have time schedules that are often a laugh because they might just as well not be there. Where buses are

Patience is a national virtue. Everywhere you will have to queue up and wait for your turn, even if you think things are not moving as fast as you would like.

supposed to run at 15-minute intervals, they more often than not come much longer in between and often three at a go. Few British seem to really mind, moan though they do, but with an almost indulgent sigh.

You soon learn to be a past master at whiling away time at the post office, bank, clinic, railway station, etc. Maybe that's why the British are mad about crossword puzzles. They really help in quelling exasperation. A little philosophy also helps. Being stuck in a 20-mile (32 kilometre) traffic jam or waiting hours for a repairman, it's good pause for reflection. It certainly makes for less stress.

THE FAMILY

The British family unit is no different from its counterpart elsewhere in the world: one, and increasingly, two working parents,

107

children (an average of two), a house or flat on mortgage and a basic social lifestyle built around the local pub, weekends and the annual two-week holiday. The rich differ only in their choice of residence location, leisure pursuits and holiday destinations: perhaps Greece or Italy instead of Torquay or Torremolinos, Disneyland instead of Brighton Pier.

The system of contributing to the family kitty is much less customary in Britain for the simple reason that financially independent young people tend to fly the coop as soon as they are able to. In this, the British are different from the Southern Europeans who still live in extended families.

When a family goes out to dinner, the bill is often split between parents and working children. Not for them, father paying for the whole family.

But the winds of change are blowing. Recent research shows that more and more single men are opting to stay at home with their parents until they set up their own families.

It has a lot to do with the cost of housing, bachelor pads being expensive, and coming home to dirty laundry and cold canned food: not exactly a warming prospect. Sceptics may say this is mother-smothering and likely to be the cause of marriage failures because of the inevitable comparison. Like 'nobody cooks like Mum does'. But whether the trend is likely to spread depends on economic factors, i.e. cost of bachelor pads, studios, and availability of services where one works and lives. The nurturing of independence away from the family fold remains the norm rather than the exception. This encourages an early maturity that can only stand the young people in good stead when they strike out on their own.

British parents are less likely than other races to be aghast if their children decide they want to 'bum' around for a bit before getting work. As long as they do not ask for handouts. The British are generally more relaxed about the need to live a useful and productive life, not wasting one minute. It's not so much indulgence as the understanding that young people have to find their own feet and direction. Spending time without actually earning money is not frowned upon as being prodigal. Many middle class parents actively encourage their grown children to explore life, soak up things if they can, especially travelling, before deciding on a job. There is much less parental pressure in this direction, unlike in more structured societies.

British youths have been accused of being indolent. While this is true to a certain extent, the few years of a teenager's life before he embarks on adulthood are often spent in the pursuit of ideals. But whatever decision he makes, deep down, every parent, especially doting mothers, would probably rather their children stay at home as long as they're not married – if there is enough room.

This philosophy applies to most British families, rich or poor, but of course the rich can be more indulgent and forgiving of their children who drag their feet about being independent. However, you read of many cases where self-reliant young people carve their own niche in life rather than live off the fat of affluent parents.

It's different kinds of society with different attitudes to what constitutes closeness and strong family ties. Close proximity does not always make for unity.

The fundamental difference in the British is that they do not subscribe to clinging. Again, it's the self-reliance factor that ultimately sees them through their twilight years.

Marriage

One in three marriages ends in divorce in Britain. But cold-blooded statistics do not take into account that many people simply do not bother with the legalities and rituals of a marriage ceremony. They simply live together and raise children.

Sociologists say that the institution of marriage in Britain has all but lost its meaning. However one has to see the situation in the contemporary light before passing judgement about moral decay. Given that laws are currently flexible in dealing with entitlements when a relationship breaks down, marriage or no marriage, young people already disenchanted with conventional and religious unions are less likely to bother about rituals and legalities.

In short, what is moral turpitude and decay to some is grist for the mill of life to the British. A young unmarried girl getting pregnant does not necessarily send her family into shock. More often than not, they are supportive and close ranks. There are few hangups about sexual infidelity and preaching about the wages of sin. Of primary concern is ultimate happiness, a realistic appraisal of what counts.

If you don't love someone any more, you leave him and you won't be tarnished as a scarlet woman. Wayward children are forgiven time and again until they go over the brink, which is sad, but it is not in the British to mete out hellfire and brimstone for something that might cause a person to be ostracised in another society.

This does not reflect that marriage as such is out of fashion – the white wedding with full trimmings is still a big business for couturiers and caterers – it reflects a rather fatalistic attitude towards life's losing dice. Many simply live together until such time they feel it imperative to make it legal. Others would hastily call it quits when a few cracks appear in their union, arguably giving up too easily rather than salvaging the marriage, and dusting off the broken pieces in order to go through the whole routine again perhaps with another partner.

So another marriage bites the dust but fewer and fewer people go into hysterics about divorce. Even with children in the middle of the trauma, husbands and wives revert to single status without too much dragged out agony. For many, the sensible attitude of remaining friends rather than bitter foes provides some balm for the children caught in between. In a strange way, this very fatalistic stance makes life easier for divorced couples to remain amicable.

It's by no means an across-the-board situation; conservative people in smaller towns probably suffer less stress because of less distraction and strain on their marriage. For a woman who is content to stay at home and child-mind while her husband brings home the bacon, there is less reason for discord or chafing at chauvinism.

For a dynamic couple in a big city, career demands often mean putting off having children, little time together and a general absence of quiet weekends. The bonds of marriage can get threadbare.

Divorce and Settlements

There is a move to make divorce even more easy than it already is. The customary period of a two-year separation as grounds for a decree is likely to be trimmed to one year. As for settlement, under the British law, the divorced woman gets half of all joint assets and the court is more likely to grant child custody to the mother, unless the court can prove she is an unsuitable mother. Maintenance and child support vary depending on the father's circumstances. Even in cases where a couple is not married, the parting of ways is not clear cut. The court can exercise the power to force the man to settle on paternity grounds, married or not.

Single Parents

Britain has an alarmingly high percentage of single parents, many of whom seem to make a go of it without too much moaning. I personally know several people whose marriages have failed but who are also determined to carry on without breaking apart. One is fiercely determined to prove she can cut it without a husband and has decided to go ahead to bring up her baby which was barely weeks old when he left her. Is she bitter? Angry? A little at first but now simply determined to make the best of her lot.

British parents are generally very supportive of their children, especially gullible daughters barely out of their teens, who get into trouble and become unmarried mothers. While statistics tell a grim story of abandoned babies (by girls as young as 14), many parents give their helpless daughters all the help they can muster without unending censure.

The Asian Indian community still holds dear their traditional values, even by those born here. Many are happy to have their marriages arranged but there have been increasing numbers of young people committing suicide rather than subject themselves to loveless marriages.

Because British children tend to be physically precocious at a young age – liberalism and relaxed mores being the major causes – they marry or enter into relationships young. Seventeen or eighteen is very common with financial security not being a problem because of the welfare state. In other words, two young people barely out of their teens play house without the attendant sense of responsibility and find they haven't got the maturity to handle relationships or parenthood. Most single parents are in this age group.

It would not be fair to pass sweeping judgement that the British are morally lax. Urban stress, disenchantment, cynicism and a general sceptical attitude about the till-death-do-us-part vow all lend to the situation. For someone brought up in a traditionally Oriental environment, it would seem a shocking state of affairs to read, daily, about relationship breakdowns, a casual attitude towards sexual indiscretions and disregard for marriage formalities.

I Just Called To Say I Love You

But the extended family does exist, perhaps not in the same way as in the East. Young people are fairly mobile in their pursuit of ambition. Leaving the family home at 18 or whatever age a young person begins to seek his niche in life is not the need for independence *per se*. The job scene may be depressed in his home town and the big city beckons with glamorous promise. So the fledgling leaves home, perhaps forever and only keeps in sporadic touch with the parents.

Sadly, many end up in the streets of big cities, especially London, seeking the proverbial pot of gold or simply hoping to get a slice of the action that was missing back home. It is easy to be critical without understanding the situation. I know that friends who see their parents once a year or even less frequently are not any less filial than children living with their parents. Nor do many of the cardboard city dwellers do so by choice. Family closeness is not measured by the yardstick of contact frequency or gestures. Some of the most loving families I have known see each other rarely – sometimes once in several years.

British parents are not inclined to hover over and smother their offspring like those in Oriental societies. Nor do they moan much about infrequent contact when the offspring leave home. I was touched by the obvious closeness of families when they did meet at Christmas and the refreshing lack of nagging from the oldsters. The old 'you don't visit often enough' moan is usually low key, if at all. Even with feeble parents who find it difficult to cope without help.

The umbilical cord gets severed quite early in life here. Children are thrust out into the world to cope even before they are out of their shorts. Like in boarding school. Whatever argument for or against, a child of eight soon learns self-sufficiency when there are no parents around to gather the loose ends. Of course you get the indulgent parents, especially with kids in day schools and living at home, but relatively few are spoilt rotten, even with wealthy families. Kids of 10 are encouraged to earn their pocket money with paper rounds or other odd jobs, even among the affluent.

Nothing Comes Free

In a country where cost of living is relatively high, earning extra pocket money does not come with any stigma. Dog-walking, baby-sitting (even for your own relatives) and Saturday clean-up jobs are taken up eagerly. Generally, British parents are careful about giving generous allowances to their children.

To this day, you will rarely see parents with young children in tow after sundown, whether to a show or a restaurant. Much less children running around the streets after dark. The odd child or two wandering the streets of London are usually the results of family breakdowns or difficult circumstances. They are soon rounded up by the police and sent home or to wherever they came from.

British males tend to marry young – the average is 22, and even younger for females, around 18. With the problem of immaturity, financial inadequacy and the arrival of children, family units forged on adolescent passion and not much else often break down. Sociologists tend to point at these circumstances when cases of child abuse are reported.

By and large, the typical family unit is one of cosy closeness with father working and mother as a home-maker, or working part-time when there is a granny around. British fathers do not generally display chauvinism, happily tackling division of labour for household and parental chores. The weekly supermarket shopping trip with mum, dad, baby in the pram and clinging toddlers paints a fairly cosy picture. For one thing, domestic help is beyond most people, barring the charlady who comes in to clean once or twice a week. The British working wife today is unlikely to let her husband get away with outright chauvinism like her sister of an earlier decade who was financially dependent on her husband.

Among many families too, there has been a trend to live in houses with the possible extension of a 'granny flat' within the premises, but yet private enough to give the old privacy and dignity. I know one couple who invited me to a champagne evening to celebrate the granting of building permission for their granny flat.

MARRYING FOR RESIDENCE

If you're a man from another country marrying a British woman, the Home Office does not automatically grant you residential status, even when you prove the marriage is genuine. Even a shared address and a joint bank account are not sufficient proof. Home Office officers do spot checks on such couples and, if residence is granted, it could be for a provisional period of one year. By and large, the Home Office is very discretionary about its decisions and not bound to explain the reason for granting or not granting residence.

Even for a foreign woman marrying a British man, residence is still not a breeze. The same rules apply, but they are more relaxed.

There has been a racket going on for years where a foreign man marries a British woman purely for residential status. Many women make a real business out of charging for such arrangements, and the press has reported many cases where a woman contracted multiple marriages, each time for thousands of pounds.

RETIREMENT

The official retirement age for men is 65 and 60 for women – though recent claims of sexual discrimination may change this difference. When they reach this time of their life, they are given their 'bus pass', an entitlement that has become something of a generic privilege much bandied about in reference to advanced years. What it means is that retirees travel free on buses (and the tube in London) and get discounts for train travel all over Britain.

Among the socially conscious tradespeople, there are schemes whereby OAPs (old age pensioners) get certain discounts. Like dry cleaning every Wednesday at half price or the cinema every Tuesday. This is not an across the board thing but practised by many in the country.

The old and infirm living in homes and in trust estates when they have families seem to reflect a certain callousness. This is not necessarily so. In many cases the old people are fiercely independent and prefer to be on their own, especially if they are couples. In some cases, the married children simply cannot accommodate them. Often young people move away from their home town by force of circumstances and their parents cannot or will not follow them.

Don't forget too that most British work until they are in their sixties, so leaving their home patch and work place is out of the

The older generation is fiercely independent and does not cling to the children for support. Many OAPs (old age pensioners) live alone and see their children and grandchildren only a few times a year.

question. Working grandparents is a norm – not an exception – among most of the working classes which constitute some 90% of the population. Even the landed gentry have to work to keep up their lifestyles and maintain their inherited premises, albeit in a different way. Running a stately home as a living (in a few cases, with decent profits) is as much hard work as any other job.

PETS
Cats

The British have long been a nation of dog lovers. Cats came a close second. However the feline tide has caught on and cat ownership now represents some £450 million a year on cat food. Even the business of feline private business rakes in some £40 million a year! More than a flavour of the month or even a fluffy Christmas present that too often got dumped when recipients went off them, cats are now pets of the moment.

Statistical forecasts have it that if every one of Britain's six million cats visits the vet once a year, vets would be £60 million richer. Feline analysts have a theory for this trend. Yuppie professionals have made them a sort of lifestyle pet – more suited to their urban stomping ground.

All you need is a cat-flap, a litter tray and you can sail blithely out of your flat without worrying about mess. You can't do this with a dog for it is not in its nature to respect the difference between a plush carpet and a mound of earth. Cats don't need to be taken for walks – a daily chore busy people have little time for. Every tom with alleycat instincts will simply vanish through his flap for his prowls and return home when satiated. Often days later.

In many a typical British suburban home, the sight of an extremely fat cat stretched out on top of the TV set, or wherever it chooses, is a cosy picture. Besotted cat owners will forgive their cats anything – even when their precious rugs are clawed to shreds.

Feline owners will go to any length to pamper their cats. Dia-

mante studded collars and cat toys are also million pound businesses. And if your tom is suffering from neuroses, refusing the designer cat food you put before him, why, there are any number of
behavioural consultants to get to the root of the problem.

Would you believe Perturbed Urban Stress Syndrome – PUSS?
Peter Neville runs a monthly clinic at the Bristol University veteri-
nary school for phobic felines.

Dogs

Much as the urban professional may love dogs, it doesn't suit his
lifestyle to have one – even a small breed. Dogs are more the old age
pensioners' devoted companions because they have all the time in
the world for endless walks, and are able to pander to the messy
nature of a weaning dog. There are about six million assorted dogs
in Britain. Many have transformed the lives of blind people, acting
as guide dogs – especially the golden retriever breed.

Dogs are used in old people's homes to comfort the elderly, are
therapeutic to the sick, and scientific tests have shown that simply
patting a dog can reduce stress.

Cats don't take kindly to being bundled in a designer tartan torso
cover – they'd rip it in seconds – and are too aloof to provide the
misty-eyed devotion which a dog can lavish on its owner.

Nonetheless it seems shocking to see an old age pensioner stinge
on her diet to feed her dog – biscuits and milk for mistress and
chopped liver and canned food for Fido. A rather unbalanced priority, but the companionship a dog can give to its owner far outweighs
the human need for more than basic sustenance.

A friend once related to me the strange lifestyle of her old age
pensioner neighbour. She was some 80 years old and devoted to her
equally mature little Yorkie Terrier. As my friend shared a common
kitchen with the old lady, she was privy to her eating habits. Every
few weeks her garbage bin would be put out and for every empty
fish finger pack there were half a dozen 'Pedigree Chum' cans. In

short she subsisted on meagre meals so that her dog could dine well on chicken, rabbit and beef.

Not too shocking a state of affairs when you consider a dog can often make the difference between a purpose in life or slow insanity. The great disparity between animal and human diets is initially astonishing. But with many old people living alone, a pet, be it a mangy cat, flea-bitten dog, goldfish or budgerigar, can provide comforting companionship and a lifeline. Many old people utterly alone slide into senile dementia much faster when faced with nothing more than four walls and fading memories. Also a barking dog can provide a sense of security when there are unwelcome visitors.

Even mongrels are not left out in the cold when it comes to dog pampering. In response to the annual dog show Crufts, which is a national showcase for pedigree dogs, some people have organised an alternative for the un-pedigreed – Scruffs. The organisation, while serious in its intent to give mongrels some media mileage, has come up with rather jokey classifications. They range from 'Dog Most Like Its Owner' to 'Lamp Post Specialist'! No doubt the haughty French poodles and Afghan hounds will look down their doggie noses at such displays.

Here are a few reasons why a dog is indispensable in alleviating a few shocks:

1. When out walking in a park in the company of a dog, you feel that much safer. At home, every dog, no matter how small, is an effective burglar deterrent.
2. Guide dogs, hearing dogs and dogs for the disabled have all been lifelines to the handicapped in Britain.
3. Meeting a fellow dog owner is one of the best ways to make friends. Canine introductions will invariably bring a smile to a British at the end of his dog lead, no matter how dour he is.
4. A dog is good for children, giving them a sense of responsibility. It also provides great companionship, especially if you live in an area where it is difficult to meet other kids.

5. Pet shops abound, should you want to own an animal that is generally in good health. And no licence is required any longer.
6. If you are less fussy about the lineage of an animal, give a home to an abandoned cat or dog of which there are thousands in animal homes. While most British are animal loving people, there are many who treat pets with callousness when they out-live their use. Or when the novelty (as in a present) wears off.

About Keeping Pets

What you must never do is to let your dog foul sidewalks. It will bring the wrath of the neighbours on your head, not to mention a likely fine. Take it for a walk in a park or any patch of grass not used as public thoroughfare.

If your dog is at all skittish about strangers, make sure it's on a lead. Most dogs in Britain are used to humans and unlikely to be snappy. In housing estates where houses have open front gardens, make sure your dog does not foul others' property if you let it loose for a run.

Vets are not expensive here and regular visits will ensure your pet keeps in good tick. Most supermarkets have a pet product counter, as prominently displayed as human consumer items.

It is NOT advisable to keep a dog in a flat – not even a little one – unless you have the time to take it out twice a day. A yapping dog in an empty house is not only a nuisance to the neighbours, it also draws attention to burglars who are professional enough to know whether your dog is a mere titch or a great fearsome hound.

Expect to spend in the region of £8 a week for animal upkeep, including medical attention, grooming and other necessities.

Unless you absolutely have no liking for animals, keeping a dog or cat in Britain is more than affluent indulgence for all the reasons mentioned above.

TRADITIONS

The reference here applies not to those of a religious or historical nature but rather those pursuits held dear to the hearts of the British. As a people, they set total store by the familiar and the security of tried and tested leisure activities. These embrace a wide spectrum from the almost-obligatory two weeks holiday a year to sport. In between, there are any number of traditions still adhered to by villages and small towns.

Pubs

An abbreviation of 'public house' with usually the host, a publican of rather sociable nature. Pubs are more than just places to drink. Each is a watering hole for devoted patrons, a bolt hole to unwind in or catch up on the latest local gossip. Many are listed as histori-

cal buildings owned by brewery chains with their names not too dis-creetly affixed under the pub's quaint hoarding. Throughout the country, you are likely to see dozens of establishments called the Crown, King's Arms, The George, The Victoria, Fox and Hound, Duke of York, or Horse and Plough. There are something like 80,000 pubs throughout the British Isles.

Age Venerated

Many pubs date back to the 15th and 16th centuries when they were private homes where the owner sold ale at his doorstep. Before the era of steam trains and cars, many such buildings became coaching inns – half-way houses for travellers to change horses and bed down after a meal and drink. But it was during the Victorian era that pubs flourished, with proprietors going over the top with glass, marble, gleaming mahogany and curlicues. Many have been lovingly restored and any that smack of modernity, chrome and steel should be given a wide berth.

Whatever the weather, however woeful the workday has been, pubs are usually packed wall-to-wall with patrons, especially on a Saturday night, intent on downing as many pints as they can before last orders. Relaxed drinking hours now mean people can drink right through the day and until midnight in some places, though 11 p.m. is the usual closing time.

And when they say 11 p.m., it usually means the shutters come down with an uncompromising clang on the dot though you may go on drinking what you have ordered before for a reasonable time.

Age of Consent

As for the age of consent, the law says you may not enter a pub if you are under 14 unless accompanied by an adult. And you may not buy alcohol if you are under 18. But the law is rarely applied. Many pubs admit whole families, toddlers and all, and rarely ask for proof of age. This is permitted by law if you are all eating.

If you are nervous about entering a pub, let alone propping yourself nonchalantly at the bar to order a beer or even an orange juice, don't be. In time, you will find it to be the kind of place where the British warm up much faster than anywhere else. The same person who greets you like a long lost friend is apt to give you the cold shoulder on a train or tube. Such is the ambience of a pub.

For a few pounds, a pub is hard to beat for a drink, social banter and getting to meet the locals. Racism rarely shows up in a pub. One can conjecture that ambience conducive to relaxed senses brings out the best in human nature. When you are in a pub, it is customary to buy a 'round' of drinks for the group of people you are with. If there are more than five or six of you, someone may offer to split the cost. You in turn will be bought a drink when others buy 'rounds'. It would seem odd, even rude, to buy yourself a drink if with friends or colleagues, or having started a conversation with a fellow drinker.

Pub Stage

When once the dart board provided an outlet for aggression and friendly competition, the plush snooker table is now an imposing fixture in the larger establishments. Others, not so privileged with space for such a clumpy piece of sports equipment, offer the 90s version of entertainment – loud music. Extremely loud music in places where the clientele is young and accustomed to ear-drum bursting hard rock.

Some places offer more refined entertainment like a resident pianist or even a full-scale musical band trying to outstage the West End with their production numbers on a postage-stamp sized stage.

Purists moan that all this defeats the purpose of a pub's function, which is to provide good brew and conversation. With changing mores and a younger pub-going population, any publican with his eye on profit will be shrewd to supply whatever is in demand.

Even more enlightening (perhaps a horrific development for serious drinkers), is that many pubs now have a section serving

An aberration for serious drinkers, the alcohol free bar is nonetheless gaining more popularity with younger professionals who enjoy the cosy ambience of a pub without the after effects of alcohol.

non-alcoholic drinks. I visited no less than half a dozen in the London area and there were as many (usually lunchtime) patrons who quite happily quaff the stuff. Young professionals take their job seriously enough not to exhale alcohol breath at an executive meeting.

Pub clientele today is largely a mixed bag where an old-age pensioner is likely to find his favourite chair occupied by a yuppie type drinking orange juice. Conversation is as likely to be peppered with the latest stock market prices as whose aunt Nellie has gout. The point is, whether you drink or not, a pub is the one place that provides a good springboard and live stage to assimilate and observe the British way of life at its most grass roots level.

Wine Bars

A fledgling establishment next to the pub, wine bars sprouted apace with the yuppie generation and are now taking their place among the serious restaurants. Just what is a wine bar? It serves wine, spirits and food – though not on a restaurant scale. In a word, a wine bar is a place to display your knowledge of wine (a relatively recent adoption among the British via their continental cousins), nibble at a quiche or sit down to an exotic Mexican, Spanish, Thai, Malaysian or Indian meal.

A rather strange assortment of gustatory pleasures but much loved by the hard-working, up-and-coming executive. It wouldn't be fair to label a wine bar as a yuppie place because it isn't. Because of the smallness of most, the atmosphere is very matey and food fast, if not silver service, and an inexpensive way to spend a convivial evening.

It is a different matter from going out to a restaurant because in a wine bar, you don't have to eat if you don't want to. Nurse a glass of house white the whole night through and the proprietor will not turn a hair. Try to do the same at a restaurant, and you will be shown the door before you can say, "Beaujolais". Herein perhaps lies its popularity given the British penchant for the grog. All the better if it has a French name because it reflects a yuppie sophistication.

There are relatively few wine bars compared to pubs and they are located mainly in the bigger towns and cities where offices abound. They offer a wide selection of wines and soft drinks, with ambience geared to small sit-down groupings. Some wine bar tables are so small that they can practically be covered by a tray! Still, patrons mind little the elbow jostling, even regarding it as chic to crouch on minuscule stools in their designer gear and chatting animatedly about the theatre. The clientele is sophisticated and cosmopolitan.

Prices are marginally lower than restaurants: you should expect to pay an average of £6 for a bottle of house wine, which you can also buy by the glass, and anything up to £35 for good champagne. Food ranges from the indifferent to good ethnic *satay*, *samosas* and even *dim sum*.

The Very Proper English Tea

Whatever else is going by the wayside, the traditional English cream tea is alive and doing very well from Cambridge to Clacton-on-Sea. Virtually every town with anything to offer visitors by way of history or natural scenic beauty boasts of at least one tea shop. For something like £4 (depending on how touristy the place is), you get a pot of tea, hot scones, home-made jam and thick cream. It is a real pick-me-up at around 4 p.m. (they serve them all hours too) and one can steep oneself in history.

Most places will have made some effort to document the history of the place, whether its Tudor architecture, for instance, or a visit by Samuel Johnson or some other literary luminary. Pretty table-cloths, dried flower arrangements and delicate bone china are *de rigueur* as are side offerings of potted jams and honey to take home. As a weekend jaunt, tearooms are lovely to soak up British history and culture, all the better if you strike up conversation with a very proper English gentlewoman who just happens to have lived in the area all her life and knows about all the skeletons in the cupboards. If it's anything that will break the traditional British reserve, it's to have a healthy curiosity for their history, murky or otherwise.

Ancient abodes seem ideally suited for this lovely tradition where you are not rushed off your feet by insolent waiters. Tearoom proprietors, especially in the country, are charming, warm, and make you feel welcome. There are hundreds of these places through-out Britain where history goes back four or five hundred years. Many still retain their original woodwork, fireplaces and atmos-phere that are as much an attraction as the brew.

For under £5 you get a real slice of British history that no fast food place can ever hope to provide.

The tearoom is a regular feature of any town or village. A hot pot of tea, delicious freshly baked scones, jam and cream: a perfect dream of pastoral gentility.

127

Doing the Country

Driving around the country is a tradition that practically every mobile British person, single or weighed down with kids and grandparents, indulges in. And one which every visitor should take every opportunity to enjoy. It's a wonderful break from weekday tedium, gets clean air into your lungs for the price of a full tank of petrol split among four, five or six, and great discoveries the tourist brochures don't tell you about.

The British Isles are literally stuffed with country places you can get to within an hour or so from wherever you happen to be.

Sheep-laden trails, trout farms, pick-your-own fruit farms and guest houses with delightfully warm proprietors are everywhere. Every county has pretty, gorgeous or at least interesting countryside to offer. It would not be fair to name any particular one as scenic

One of the joys of driving through the country is stumbling upon charming little villages where the pace of life is slower than in the cities.

beauty is in the eyes of the beholder.

Do not expect, however, a wide choice of eating places with at most a pub, teashop or hamburger stall. Hot dog stands can be found along many roads and dual carriageways but the shock comes in waxy sausages, dreadful tea and greasy onions. You're better off buying a punnet of strawberries or whatever fruit is in season.

Bed and Breakfast

The British tradition of offering bed and breakfast for a nominal price of £25 to £45 per night (this varies depending on season, type of place, etc.) is the visitor's best friend. Outside large towns and cities, hotels are a rarity. Country folk who turn their homes into B&B places are a far cry from formal hotel staff. They're warm, friendly and go to great lengths to make your stay comfortable even for one night.

Don't expect the plush amenities of a hotel. Your room will be basic, cosy, clean and probably full of personal artefacts. Quite likely, the owner's son has had to give up his room for the family's extra income.

Often, you will join the family for dinner – at a nominal cost, of course. But it is the breakfast that warms most visitors.

Most B&B places can accommodate several families and you will have the pleasure of company for the traditional meal of sausages, eggs, toast, tea and jam, all included in the price. Lately, as a gesture to American tourists, many places have begun to serve cereal and fruit as well.

But there is nothing more glorious than being served a hot breakfast of sausages, eggs sunny side up, hot toast, fragrant jam or marmalade while looking out onto a pastoral scene. There are literally hundreds of these places in every province and at least several in small villages. Apart from in high summer, they are not usually full, but half the fun is in stumbling upon a charming picture-post-card farmhouse with a beckoning sign on B&B vacancies.

CUSTOMS AND CELEBRATIONS

City dwellers the world over are inclined to be blasé about age-old customs and the British urbanite is no different. But those in rural Britain are less dismissive of traditional lore that makes a welcome change to their daily routine; a refreshing anchor even for hard-boiled city people, in a rapidly changing world. For one thing these traditions are not as transient as the latest hip hop. For another, most British people have their roots in a rural and agricultural past.

Many traditions have links with what were regarded by the Church as 'heathen' practices. They were pagan rites that became inextricably entwined with Christian festivals. Christmas, in all its present joyousness, came from a mixture of Roman pagan cults and the heathen Germanic mid-winter feast of 'Yule'. In Roman times the week preceding Christmas was a 'Saturnalia' of debauchery.

Many traditions evolved from superstition, and despite rationality and Christianity, the British still consider certain things taboo. They may enter into the spirit of things for sheer novelty and fun but would not dismiss some superstitions lightly.

Not all British traditions have ancient roots though. Certain festivals were nurtured from Victorian times onwards but all have been perpetuated by that most pervasive of media – television. Paradoxically, this house-bound passive pastime is seen as a potential destroyer of traditions expressed via communal outdoor activity.

At least for a foreigner who may not have the opportunity to observe, much less participate in, a folksy tradition unfolding on television in glorious colour in his living room helps him to understand the British better. Passive it may be, but still an absorbing way to enrich one's knowledge of a foreign culture. It makes for much better understanding of the people, all the better when you do not have an opportunity to participate in a particular ritual.

To chronicle them all would take a massive tome, suffice to know what the more popular and visible ones are in the British festival calendar and what they're all about.

New Year's Day

New Year celebrations explode in vast public gatherings in Edinburgh, Glasgow and London. Every noise-making paraphernalia you can think of joins in a tremendous cacophony as thousands link arms to sing *Auld Lang Syne*, everyone is boozed to the gills, kissing liberally and the church bells peal in ear-splitting unison. The London Trafalgar Square celebrations are most famous. Something like a million people are crushed together with quite a few casualties at the end of the day after. If you dare to brave this human quagmire, ushering in the New Year in Britain is an unforgettable event.

There are many superstitions attached to New Year's Day in northern England and Scotland. It is believed that nothing must be removed from the house and people refuse to lend anything to neighbours until 2nd January. It is the firmly held belief that the New Year must begin happily, luckily and after a clean break with the past. Hence the practice of resolutions which, today, is generally the result of the season's over-indulgence and lasts only till its aftermath! In Scotland, if the first person who sets foot in someone's house is tall and dark, he is believed to bring good luck. In Yorkshire and Lincolnshire, fair men are the harbingers of good fortune. But if you have flat feet, are lame, cross-eyed or have eyebrows that meet in the middle – don't on any account step into someone's home on New Year's Day. Of course only the superstitious will take all this seriously, but as a foreigner, it is always more prudent to be aware of likely gaffes. If you want to be invited back.

Easter

The most revered of all Christian festivals, it celebrates the Resurrection of Christ from the dead, on the first Sunday following the 21st of March after the full moon. Because of lunar variability, Easter can be anywhere between 22 March and 25 April. All devout Roman Catholics and Anglicans attend church and receive holy communion.

Many traditions dating back to ancient times are still observed at Easter, but mainly in rural areas. Others are apt to use the four-day holiday to get away from it all – including church! In fact the Friday before Easter is one mad scramble throughout the country when people try to get away to their favourite resorts, spas or country cottages. Road, rail, sea and air routes are usually choked!

As for the Easter egg, which is an ancient symbol of new life and spring awakening that became attached to the festival, its 20th century role seems to be quite removed from reflecting the Resurrection. Traditionally given away for good luck after being ceremonially blessed, Easter eggs today are chiefly remarkable for supporting the chocolate industry. Creamed, coated, beribboned and otherwise jazzed up to make cute, elegant or zany presents, they reflect little of the religious significance. Manufacturers and confectionery shops are less bothered with their raison d'être than that they roll in the cash.

April Fool's Day – 1 April

I have never seen a people go to such great lengths in national leg-pulling! The British penchant for 'send ups' is in top gear on this day and the media, especially, pull out all the stops. One year a national daily ran the story of a master plan to move Trafalgar Square several hundred yards from its present site. Hundreds of people turned up to watch the titanic engineering feat! Of course the whole thing was a monumental hoax.

A BBC television programme devoted much time and effort to put one over the public. In dead seriousness, the presenter came on to say an unearthly creature had been discovered on the misty slopes of the Himalayas by archeologists. This 'Lirpa Loof' had a blue body, funny ears and excreted purple turds! The discovery was then caged in London Zoo and the cameras were there to record public curiosity and befuddlement. And the BBC never explained their cheeky hoax.

This licensed mischief, believed to be derived from the irreverent Roman Saturnalia, flourishes from boundless ingenuity of perpetrators all over the country. There is a curious rule that binds the mirth-making. At noon, all jokes must cease or the hoax rebounds on the jester.

Halloween

The 31st of October is All Souls' Day, when in olden days witches were believed to meet and plot together. Today American style 'tricks or treat' visits of small children, often wearing masks or fancy dress, are becoming more frequent in large towns. In order to avoid anything nasty from happening, keep a bag of sweets or some small change handy if you are home on 31 October.

The State Opening of Parliament

Even within the small square of a television set, the State Opening of Parliament in October or November is a not-to-be-missed spectacle. British Parliament is more than 700 years old and in this time has developed complex and grand customs and ceremonies second only to the monarchy in opulence.

On the evening before the opening, cellars of the Palace of Westminster are ceremonially searched by Yeomen of the Guard with light from candle lanterns. It is believed to date back to 1605 when a similar search uncovered the infamous Gunpowder Plot perpetrated by Guy Fawkes (see below).

Two processions then set out from Buckingham Palace, each with a mounted escort of Household Cavalry. One carries the crown in its own gilded coach, guarded by the Royal Watermen. The second procession comprises the Queen and her family. At 11 a.m. the monarch, now with her crown and in her parliament raiment, leads the way to the House of Lords to assume her throne. Her messenger, known as Black Rod, then summons the members of the House of Commons. He knocks three times with his black rod and then conveys his message. Historically, since 1641, no member of Royalty has entered this lower chamber in person, symbolising the disastrous attempt by Charles I to arrest the Five Members. The monarch then reads her speech which, in reality, is an announcement of the government's political programme.

There are many curious customs but none more so than that governing tobacco. No MP may smoke during Parliament but they may take snuff. This is contained in the House of Commons Snuff Box, made of wood taken from the chamber destroyed by bombs in 1941. It is kept by the Principal Door-keeper. Members also have the right to stop all traffic while crossing the road to the House. At the end of each ordinary session of Parliament, members cry out "Who goes home?" echoing the days when members banded together under armed guard each night before setting off home.

Guy Fawkes Day

On 5 November 1605, a plot to blow up the Houses of Parliament was discovered and its perpetrators apprehended and hanged. Ever since, it has been a great tradition to celebrate Guy Fawkes Day and the continuation of parliamentary government by building and then burning a huge bonfire. Models of effigies of Guy Fawkes, called 'guys', are made beforehand and burned on the bonfires, generally with a fireworks display which echoes the exploding of gunpowder.

You will often see small children collecting money for fireworks with a ragged 'guy', outside London tube stations, in shopping precincts and near supermarkets. They will call "Penny for the Guy" – but will sneer if you give less than 10 or 20 pence. Many boroughs give a public bonfire and fireworks display, either on 5 November or on the nearest Saturday, using money from local rates to entertain their residents and also hoping to limit the annual accident rate as individuals injure themselves with fireworks and fire brigades throughout the country are stretched to full capacity.

Christmas

25 December is the date of the Roman Winter Solstice with the celebration dating back to the 4th century after Christianity became the state religion of Rome. By then it had adopted aspects of popular pagan cults, like debauchery and drinking to bacchanalian excess. In the 10th century Christmas adapted many customs from the German heathen practices of Yule and by the 11th century all the elements were synthesised into a recognisable Christ's Mass.

Sword dancing, wassailing and yule logs were heathen practices condemned by the Protestant Reformation. In Scotland, puritanical Calvinists suppressed all public Christmas celebrations and till this day the New Year is celebrated with more fervour than Christmas.

It was in 1840 that Prince Albert and Charles Dickens pioneered the great sentimentality, traditionalism and the Christmas spirit embodied in the classic literary work *A Christmas Carol*. Who has read this heart-tugging story and not been moved by the pathos of it all? Thus the Victorian Christmas set the stage for present day celebration.

Christmas Cards

The Victorian age also witnessed the start of Christmas cards, the first being the work of one Henry Cole in 1846. In Britain today, more than a billion cards are printed and sent out all over the world, giving the post office a nightmare from August onwards. You'd be wise to send your cards no later than the second week of December if you expect them to arrive in time.

Presents

The giving of presents dates from mid-Victorian times when it was the custom to give them to servants and children. Until then presents were given out on New Year's Day and Twelfth Night. Much of this has diffused and people give presents on Christmas Day itself or just beforehand. The stores are a veritable Aladdin's cave of gift items from October onwards, with gift vouchers now an accepted part of the tradition.

Christmas Decorations

Some people deem it unlucky to put decorations up, especially evergreens, before Christmas Eve. They have links with mid-winter rites pre-dating Christianity, and are therefore pagan. Holly, ivy and mistletoe are believed to be magical plants bearing fruit during the season when everything else is dead. The berries of the holly are believed to ward off witchcraft as they represent Christ's blood and its spines his crown of thorns. Ivy symbolises immortality but mistletoe is dismissed by churches as a pagan heritage. Its survival is largely attibuted to the home practice of hanging a branch above a doorway so people can kiss anyone passing under it without fear.

Most revered is the Christmas tree popularised by Prince Albert in 1840 and which became the much-loved centrepiece of Christmas celebrations in every British family. What with the plastic age we live in, artificial trees inevitably make the scene but most British will try to buy a really nice, fresh uprooted conifer for their living room.

But by the Twelfth Night every vestige of the evergreen centrepiece must be removed – indeed every trace of Christmas bunting – or the household will be blighted with bad luck.

Changing of the Guard

At 11.00 a.m. each day in summer and alternate days in winter, bearers of the Queen's Regimental Colour from St James Palace march down the Mall to join the Buckingham Palace detachment. This symbolises the changing of the old and new – St James is the oldest established royal residence – and at 11.30 the ceremony begins. The retiring guard hands over the palace keys and the new sentries take their posts with military stamping and slow music. It is a brilliant visual experience reflecting the pomp and pageantry of royal lifestyle, with the guards in bearskin helmets and scarlet coats. The public take delight in trying to make the sentries twitch or move a muscle. They are trained not to do so and nothing, not even a nosy camera inches from their nostrils, will produce a quiver.

Fairs

One of the most English of all traditions, fairs spring up at the drop of a hat. Annually there are something like 8000, some little village affairs and others spread over a whole county. Whatever their traditional history, fairs are for the most part an excuse for merrymaking, eating and, of course, drinking.

Until the 19th century the majority of fairs were commercial exercises – markets for goods, farm produce and animals. Then,

Country fairs retain a touch of medieval pageantry. In the past, they played an essential role in trade and socialisation.

137

only large towns had shops in the modern sense and a fair meant a shopping spree for people living in remote places. They could stock up on meat and other staples while having a nice day out.

Every village, town, borough and even a housing estate holds some sort of fair at least once a year, especially in summer. Some are no more than a collection of stalls selling anything from *samosas* to home-made jams while others will feature very loud bands. Each becomes a platform for local residents to gather, make acquaintances and spread community spirit. It is at these functions that you find the traditional British reserve melting.

BRITISH POLITICS

British Parliament is divided into two chambers – the House of Lords and the House of Commons. The House of Lords still has important powers but it is the Commons that is the main legislature where laws are passed. In practice the legislative powers are in the hands of the government because it controls the majority party in the Commons. The Commons does not pick a government but maintains it by party organisation. Its work is also to question and criticise the government's actions. The House of Commons is really an arena where political parties fight their major battles and thrash out issues of public concern. Through its debates, questions and passage of Bills, the public is made aware of politics, especially through the media. The highest positions in British politics are normally obtained after a long apprenticeship in the Commons. After this, any ministerial post is within grasp – even Number 10 Downing Street. For many MPs, it could be a job for life, especially as there are relatively few landslide elections where a large number of seats change hands.

The House of Lords

This is the second chamber of British Parliament. More than 1100 peers are entitled to take part in its proceedings but the daily average attendance is around 300. Historically, it was a power-base and even as important as the Commons. The stark contrast between its members of hereditary peerage, overwhelmingly Conservative, led to its gradual loss of power and reform. In 1958 life peerage was created, which broke the hereditary principle and also allowed women to become members. But, unlike Commons MPs, peers receive no salary – only an attendance allowance and travelling expenses.

The Lords is part of the legislature, with all Bills passing through it. It sits for about 36 weeks a year but debates lack the drama of the Commons where key political figures of each party are found. Every party has its own leader in the Lords, the Chief Whip who organises the parliamentary procedures to maximise party support. But the Lords also has a number of 'crossbench' peers who do not belong to any party.

The Lords debates on issues of current importance backed by the wide range of experience and knowledge of peers who have reached the top of their professions. They may or may not make much difference to public opinion, but are widely reported and have a way of exerting pressure on the government and raising public issues. There are those who believe there is no necessity for a second chamber in Parliament, especially one tilted firmly on the side of the Conservatives. Also, inherited privilege, tradition and the existence of titles themselves reinforce a class system that egalitarians feel Britain could well do without.

Two-Party System and Others

Britain has only had Labour or Conservative governments since 1945. The majority of the people vote for one or the other though there have been many parties since the middle of this century.

• The Conservative Party developed in the 1830s with right wing leanings and active support for free enterprise, individual initiative, reduction of government expenditure and hence taxation, competition and choice. Firmly 'establishment' with support tra-

139

ditionally from the middle and upper classes, it nonetheless has been responsible for many social reforms.

The Conservatives, cautious about changes, hence the name, came into power again under Margaret Thatcher in the 1980s. The previous Labour government had nationalised a large number of industries and suffered a series of demoralising labour strikes, and the same party had introduced the National Health Service in the late 1940s. The Conservatives undertook a massive programme of putting these industries back into private hands and attempts were made to make the NHS more financially accountable and efficient. The continued existence of private schools and medicine underscores the belief that people have a right to choose how they want to spend their money.

The media frequently refers to the Conservatives as the 'Tory' party. This is an alternative name inherited from the former English right-wing political party in existence since the 17th century.

- The Labour Party claims to represent the interests of the working classes (as against capitalism) and was first formed at the end of the 19th century mainly out of trade union amalgamation. This was the Labour Representation Committee to work for the election of MPs who would represent working people in Parliament independent of the other parties. It went on to win 29 seats in the House of Commons, effectively replacing the Liberal Party as the main opposition to the Conservatives, and in 1924 the first Labour government was formed.

The Labour Party and trade unions are generally referred to as two branches of the 'Labour Movement'. Traditional support comes from urban and highly industrialised areas, but middle class support for Labour is by no means insignificant today.

- The Liberal Party was a major political force in the late 19th and early 20th century that campaigned actively for the freedom of thought and action. They were a serious threat to the Conservatives, but the Labour Party usurped their popularity in the 1920s.

It was Britain's third largest party until 1980. In 1981, they entered into an alliance with the newly formed Social Democratic Party and two years later received the highest votes for a third party since 1920. In 1987 they became officially the SLD Party or popularly the Democrats.

- The Communist party of Great Britain was founded in 1920 by left-wing forces with two objectives: to counter the threat of world war and combat the power of commercial monopolies. It did not have much success as a parliamentary party and membership has steadily declined. It is believed there are some 10,000 members today.

- The Green Party, founded in 1973 under the name of the Ecology Party, campaigns vociferously for a nuclear-free society. It took the green name in 1985 in line with other European green parties fighting the same causes. Not represented in the Commons, it nevertheless has a growing support list.

- Plaid Cymru (Party of Wales) is the nationalist party formed in 1925 to campaign (and it is still campaigning) for the separation of Wales from the United Kingdom. The Welsh are fiercely proud of their culture and ancient Celtic language, and fear an eventual erosion if they are not preserved.

- The Scottish National Party (SNP) has the same campaign stand as Plaid Cymru. Founded in 1928, its popularity has waxed and waned. It is currently very active in parliamentary contests.

Elections and Voting

By the Parliamentary Act of 1911, an election must be called within five years of the last one. When exactly is the Prime Minister's decision and few PMs have waited the full five years, calling for a general election when 'the time is ripe'. Voting is not compulsory, and everyone who is over 18 is allowed to vote. If the government is defeated, the Prime Minister resigns and the leader of the new majority party is invited by the Queen to form a new government.

Chapter Seven

INTEGRATING INTO BRITISH SOCIETY

MANNERS

You are likely to encounter totally different types of manners as a foreigner first thrust amid British mores. Whether asking someone for directions, dealing with service staff or simply passing the time of day with a fellow passenger can be fascinating insights into the spectrum of British manners.

A working class chap will answer, "Don't know, mate" when asked for directions. And likely as not, with a cheery smile and an accent reflective of his roots, be it northern, cockney or Welsh.

On the one hand, there are the working classes who believe in a back-slapping bonhomie that precludes the need to mind one's Ps and Qs. And still come across as warm, friendly people. On the other, the posh middle classes who breathe refinement could imbue politeness with a cold superciliousness.

You see this contrast all the time in Britain. The great divide between a ruddy-cheeked innkeeper in the country and the forbidding, sullen mien of a concierge in a posh hotel can be a chasm. Perhaps they act from the basis of their trade's requirements. Manners are usually the result of upbringing and education.

Which is not to say which set of manners is right or wrong. Just different. You might find the rough and ready manners of the street stall holder more enchanting than the upper class ooze of mellifluous diction. Your bed and breakfast landlady can be all charm in her barking admonitions to her staff.

Yet, a housekeeper at a three-star hotel who says, "Hortense, the linen on the breakfast table this morning left a lot to be desired" could strike fear into the hearts of cowering chambermaids. Both have the same desired effect but it speaks volumes for the difference in tone and possible effects on others.

Neither is it true any more that the well-mannered do not swear or otherwise employ salty language. They just do it with sharper articulation and more linguistic pungence. You hear much the same thing, saltier even, in every pub and bus stop.

Some boisterous members of the upper classes seem bent on destroying their patina of refinement with a vengeance. When a titled lady called an airport staff 'a silly cow', it made headlines for days. The insult is traded everyday in the supermarket, the street and homes, and nobody turns a hair. You see, it's not so much what manners are employed but your station in life that dictates how it is perceived. In short, when invited to a home you know to be fairly refined and privileged (by virtue of money, title, etc.) you'd have to watch your language or risk never being asked again.

In the home of a humble person not given to any sort of pretension, you take the cue from his behaviour. Not to mean you can be rude, but the odd 'silly bugger or cow' in jokey reference is less likely to turn a hair.

How to Behave as a Guest

When invited to tea, no matter what your host's station in life, you should observe a certain etiquette. It can only reflect well on you. When given tea, do not clank your spoon vigorously. Always pour milk in first, then add sugar. Sip quietly. And don't hold the cup with the palm of your hand as if cradling it. Hold it by the handle with your thumb and forefinger, with the saucer in your other hand.

Having a meal with the family in the kitchen is a most enjoyable experience, particularly if it is in an old country home.

Dinner can be a problem if you are unfamiliar with the mode of eating. You can be disarmingly honest and profess to be ignorant, and chances are any clumsiness will be indulged with amusement. Or you can observe what your host is doing and mirror the actions.

Expect some time to be spent on pre-dinner drinks and light conversation. It is increasingly a trend for people to pile into the nearest pub for drinks. This is sensible as it saves the host or hostess the bother of washing up innumerable glasses. It is also an opportunity to be amid a typical British ambience. Don't refuse to go along, even if you don't drink. Nurse an orange juice for an hour if you have to. Weekend social occasions of this kind tend to operate on flexi-time and many a time I had to quell my stomach rumbling because my hosts did not seem to want to make a move about food!

If it's a buffet, wait to be asked by the host before you dig in or when handed a plate. And do not sit on the floor, even if the home is small and there doesn't seem to be enough chairs around. Stand and eat and find a handy counter – fireplace mantel or occasional table – for your drinks. Do not insist on helping with the washing up if the host demurs when you offer. Some people are averse to relative strangers in their kitchens.

Unless you're with very good friends, ask before you use the telephone, bathroom, etc. Don't, whatever you do, blunder about opening doors and poking into private quarters. The British are particularly averse to people doing this or asking them the price of artefacts in the home. If asked to be an overnight guest, abide by whatever is laid on for you, even if asked to sleep on a couch. Most people who have overnight guests often have a sofabed. Come breakfast time, change into proper clothes. It is simply not done to eat in your pyjamas unless it's with close friends.

In a Shop

You'll rarely see sales persons hovering around unless it's a small shop. Peruse till you find what you want and then go to the checkout counter. Or ask if what you want is not on view or in a different size not displayed. Most shops have expensive things like leather goods wired to electronic alarms; so if you want to try something on, don't simply pull it off the rack.

Chain stores like Marks & Spencer dot the high street of every town in the country. You pick up what you want to buy and pay at the counter.

In a Restaurant

Always state your name if you have a reservation and wait to be seated. Do not walk in and find your own table – even in the humblest place. Restaurants dislike this as they have their seating plans worked out for reserved places. Don't clank your cutlery for attention. The ratio of waiting staff to customers in Britain is not very high and some waiting is inevitable. They will get to you in time. Unbecoming behaviour will only cause waiters to either ignore you or to be rude. Don't make repeated orders for different things at different times. They would rather you take your time and give it all to them in one go. It is now illegal for restaurants to put a mandatory tip on the bill though some still do it. The customary amount is 10% of the total and it is at the customer's discretion. If you should refuse to tip, you are within your legal rights but do not make a fuss. Simply say that the service wasn't up to scratch and leave quietly.

At a Pub

As patronage is usually brisk at pubs, often two or three deep on weekends, wait patiently at the bar counter till served. It's not done to barge your way in through other customers or rap the counter for attention. Depending on the bar staff, you might get a rude response.

THE RULE AT WORK

Aside from working in an industry in which you are ensconced among people of your own nationality or at least of the same cultural background, adapting to the British working environment can be a little difficult. Sensitivities can be inadvertently rubbed the wrong way. Whatever the level of insidious racism, imagined or real, degree of acceptance and inter-cultural bonhomie, being one of a few minority can be at first uncomfortable.

Given the general nature of most British, colleagues, while welcoming you to the firm, often still remain fairly aloof. Make the first tentative steps by asking to be guided into the firm's machinations. You probably know what to do already, but the 'foreigner asking for help' bit is an essential exercise in this instance. A simple 'Where is the best place to eat?' will often garner response from those genuinely keen to help you settle in. If you start by loping off alone on your tea or lunch break, chances are you will not be welcomed into their bosom for a while. It's making your colleagues feel you have every intention of being one of the team: appealing to their sense of being the national host to your guest status. At least that's what you are technically and hopefully not for too long before cultural differences disappear in an atmosphere of professional brotherhood.

Don't be anti-social even if you are disinclined to have 'one for the road' after work. This latter is a big thing in any sizable office where staff wind down for various reasons. One is to avoid the rush hour traffic and the other is simply to enjoy a pint or two outside the workaday pressures. It's a wonderful chance for colleagues to get to know each other on a personal level. No one is saying you should take up drinking if it's against your inclination. It's the inter-relationship possible only outside office hours and that can put you on a firmer path to being accepted.

Don't forget that there could be some distrust in a few British who themselves may not have been exposed to foreigners before. Don't see it as bloodymindedness – simply ignorance and lack of exposure to alien mores. The way you speak, what you wear, eat, and how you conduct yourself could be strange to most of your colleagues, and vice versa. Start on this premise and make an effort to explain anything that jars within your adopted environment.

If it is compulsory to wear a suit and tie, do so. Bucking the system on personal grounds, like you hate ties or you never wear suits, isn't being positive. Most establishments, be it a supermarket or bank, have house rules and refusing to comply is being bloody-minded. As for office politics, depending on how crucial your position is in the pecking order and whether your survival depends on it, the cardinal rule is never get involved unless your job depends on it. There is no yardstick for this battleground – only one of integrity. If you are falsely accused of being political just because your attitude towards your boss may be different, try and explain it. You may come from a culture that teaches absolute respect for seniors, therefore your behaviour towards them may seem overly servile. This could be misinterpreted. If everybody addresses the boss by his first name, do likewise, whatever your culture teaches you. Remember, you have to adapt to them – not the other way round.

SETTING UP A BUSINESS

Your local *Yellow Pages* has a listing of business and management consultants who, even if they cannot help your particular needs, will direct you to the relevant government or local council agencies. Many firms will give you all the help you need in presentations to banks and financial institutions, how to get a government grant, taxation and corporate structures. One of the biggest firms dealing in business and financial advice is Price Waterhouse which has offices all over the country. Other firms deal with the training of staff, market research and analyses.

It would be foolish to set up business in a foreign country without seeking the advice of people who know the rules. If you are applying for residence on the premise of setting up a business, the Home Office will give you the guidelines. Basically, you have to set up a business worth about £250,000 and only if the type of business is approved by the Home Office. There are categories of businesses which are saturated and therefore an application will be a waste of time. The Home Office will be able to tell you what these are.

Once approved, you have to give employment to at least two locals and pay wages according to the national minimum guidelines. Should you want to employ someone from overseas who may have a skill you cannot find locally, you have to advertise in a relevant newspaper and prove this fact to the Home Office.

He or she will then be given a work permit, renewable every year for four years. After this, your employee may apply for permanent residence subject again to Home Office approval. There is no automatic granting of permanent residence under any category – and there are many. Check with the Home Office.

Be prepared for bureaucracy with the different authorities – especially Health. You have to satisfy many requirements – some of which may seem pointless to you, but the British are sticklers for rules and regulations. For example, if you are setting up a factory for food production, there is a quagmire of regulations. One is that

149

you may not use the same sink for food processing and hand washing. It seems impractical but it is a hard and fast rule. Fire exits in your premises are another sticky area, whatever your business may be. Because of the weather and constant draughts, doors have to be shut all the time. Therefore, in case of fire, there must be adequate exits as specified by the Fire Department.

When it comes to dealing with staff, suppliers, clients and other business contacts, there are a few cardinal rules to remember.

Suppliers

Expect weeks rather than days for things to be done, especially in office fittings and appliances installations. Be precise about what you want. Most fitters and engineers take orders from a central office and will not deviate, should you dither over where you want this or that to be permanently sited. It could cost you a lot in time and money if you don't have a firm plan of action. Always ask for several quotes and look for hidden extras like transport charges, call out fees and overtime. Few British workers are given to flexible give and take. An hour overtime is an hour overtime.

Very often the person who instals your equipment will not be authorised to collect money. You will be invoiced by the firm's head office which can be in a totally different part of the country. If you are dissatisfied with the service, the installations person may not be the person to complain to. Like if the equipment sent is incorrect. Always speak to the head office and be prepared to wait days or even weeks before the problem can be rectified. Most big suppliers have specific days on which they deliver and instal.

Staff and Wages

Expect to pay a receptionist/stenographer in the region of £7000 a year gross. The employers pay the tax which is around 30% and national insurance. Most workers are PAYE, or Pay As You Earn, and they take home money generally on a weekly basis after taxes.

Every worker is entitled to two weeks' sick pay and an average of two weeks' paid holiday per year. Also employees are not required to present a medical chit if they are sick for less than three days. If you advertise for staff, you may not stipulate the gender or nationality of would-be applicants as it is against the law, unless you have special circumstances which can overrule this.

Communication

Public service offices are notoriously overburdened with enquiries and every call you make is generally held on queue – sometimes for as long as half an hour – before it is answered. Be patient. Ringing off and trying again will put you back at the end of the queue. Don't be impatient when you are put on hold. This is a fairly big country with departmental divisions that handle specific enquiries. Unless you can be specific, your call may be routed a bit before you get to the person you want to speak to. Don't bark at the person at the other end who may not seem to understand your needs. If you explain clearly, you will usually get some help and re-direction.

RENTING ACCOMMODATION
Service Flats

It is not advisable to arrive in Britain for any extended stay without making prior arrangements for accommodation. Nor is buying a house sight unseen. So rental makes the most sense for the first few months. Chances are you will not be able to organise this straight away, so it's best to stay in serviced accommodation (unless you have friends who can put you up for a few weeks) until you sort it out. Check if there are agencies in your home country which can do this for you. Generally, in Central London, expect to pay upwards of £500 a week depending on the locality. In Greater London (as a rough guide, this is the area outside the Circle Line on the Underground map) you can get a two or three-bedroom flat with basic amenities for cooking and laundry for about £200 a week.

Houses

These can be quite expensive, especially in Central London and in affluent counties. Some estate agents (there is one in virtually every high street of every town in Britain) will have a list of houses for rental if the area you choose to live in has a largish foreign community. You cannot rent council accommodation until you establish residence and, in any case, there is a long waiting list.

If you are renting through an agency – in most cases it is best to leave all the paperwork to them – you are less likely to run into problems with the landlord. Agents will only handle premises that pass muster and provide comfortable and well-oiled facilities. If you rent on your own through local advertisements, landlords can be elusive creatures and when utility services break down, you could wait a while before they get fixed. Saving a little money by renting thus – agents' fees are added to your weekly rent – could cause more headaches than you bargained for. Many houses in Britain are old and problems arise with cold weather. Rising damp, frozen pipes, condensation and chilling draughts are just a few likely gremlins.

A house usually comes with a garden and the maintenance required to keep it from becoming a grubby patch. Unless you want to undertake this yourself, make sure that it is mentioned in the contract that it is the landlord's responsibility. Few landlords want to do this for obvious reasons. It is invasion of your privacy and not a logistical exercise. If you haven't done gardening before, a trip to a garden centre will soon set you on the right path and you'll discover the joys of this most British pursuit.

What the landlord should undertake is the maintenance of your central heating system and other utilities, should they go on the blink. Leave no area uncovered: who supplies cleaning materials, electric bulbs, extra heaters, laundry of drapes and other non-personal haberdashery. Once a contract is signed, a landlord cannot evict you on any grounds before the period of stay expires. What is important is a harmonious agreement whereby your landlord is

A garden requires care and maintenance. But nothing beats the joy of plucking the sun-ripened fruit from the tree or shrub.

accessible and amiable about certain grey areas. For example, if you cause a breakdown of your washing machine, who pays for the repairs? In most cases, professional landlords will have adequate long-term maintenance contracts for such equipment. Apply this to all electrical appliances to make sure each is covered by an extended warranty. You will only have to phone the service engineers. Also, does your bill cover the cost of utilities? If so, up to how much? Telephone bills are always the responsibility of the tenant.

Rents for houses vary greatly depending on the locality. A three-bedroom cottage in Wales may cost a mere £150 a week and a small two-bedroom terrace in Central London £1000. You decide on your budget and narrow down the choice within the area you want.

Flats

These are less expensive (again depending on location) but basic rental guidelines still apply. For instance a posh two-bedroom flat in London's Mayfair could cost up to £800 a week. What you get is the privilege of living among the affluent classes, perhaps a porter and 24-hour security. Or a bedsit in Scotland for £80 a week where you share a common toilet and tiny kitchen.

In the suburbs, flats are much less expensive if they are basic. There are not that many high rises in Britain outside the cities as the British are generally averse to apartment living. If you do find a flat that suits your needs, go through it with a fine tooth comb. Are the electrics sound? Is there double glazing, central heating, well-lagged boiler and immersion heater? The latter is a backup hot water system if the gas should be turned off for any reason.

Unlike in a house where you are buffered against noisy or difficult neighbours, flat-living comes with some problems that are best avoided. Check who or what your neighbours are like, not just next door, but below and above you. Transport, banking, school and other facilities must be looked into for their proximity if you don't own a car.

Who pays for what is again crucial in the area of repairs, carpets and maintenance. Under the law, all tenants pay their own community charge (poll tax) though this tax is likely to change (see page 20). Depending on the borough or county, it varies from under £200 to a high of £600 per person per year. Whether your contract takes this in as the landlord's responsibility is subject to agreement, but few landlords will agree to this. Generally flats go for an average of £60 per room counting living and dining areas. In other words, a two-bedroom flat with sitting and dining rooms will cost around £240 a week. But there are too many variables in a country as diverse as Britain where property prices range so widely. In the depressed areas, you could probably get a whole mansion for the same price as a flat in London – if it is in a fit state to live in. The common nightmare among flat tenants in Britain, especially in the urban areas, is the lack of regular maintenance. When you rent direct from landlords, especially in a large house converted into many small flats, the chances are they are only interested in the revenue and not much else.

Rooms

These are even more difficult to find in any major city with a thriving economy. Most are rented out on a direct first-come first-served basis without agents and you negotiate directly with the landlord. The best kind of room to rent for single people is that in a house where the family lives. Perhaps a child has grown up and now lives away and the family needs the extra income, even the company of another human being if it's a single aged parent.

The amount of rent again varies, but generally a room cannot be had for less than £40 a week inclusive of amenities, but not the phone bill. Most landlords in this situation will ask you to fill in your book of say 10p every time you make a local call and then pay him a lump sum every quarter when the phone bill arrives.

Renting such a room is more hassle-free and, as long as you pay your rent regularly, you are pretty much left on your own. But check that you do have the run of the house, use of the kitchen or whatever the landlord stipulates. Take nothing for granted – even watching TV in his sitting room. Check first that your agreement covers this.

Most room tenants provide their own cutlery, utensils, etc, unless the landlord has offered you the use of his equipment. The cardinal rule with living in a rented room, as opposed to a flat or house, is abide by the house rules. You may be asked to help out in vacuuming the house once a week, do the laundry or generally upkeep the areas where you have common use.

Are you allowed visitors and to what extent? Who provides such basics as toilet paper, detergents, etc.? No area is too small to cover for it pays in the long run to clarify household expenditure. Ask for a rent book and agree on the amount of deposit (against breakages) and advance. The norm is two weeks' deposit and two weeks' advance.

Last but not least, should you run into major problems, contact your local citizens advisory bureau who can help you sort out legal and other matters of unfair treatment. Your local council office will have the telephone number and address.

MONEY, CONVERSION

Probably the most reverberating and with the furthest-reaching effect, right through your pocket, is the shock encountered when converting any currency into sterling.

My constant moan in the early years in England was the unbelievable price of everything, especially after I converted every single penny I spent. If you have a creed to live by anywhere in England, it must be this: don't convert, or go home. Unless it's in your favour. But it is not usually the case.

In your first few months, you are apt to convert every penny you spend, especially on consumer goods and moan about the relative cost of everything. One lesson I learnt was not to insist on having things I used to have in Singapore. Everything imported is a premium product, especially if it has to travel thousands of miles. Imported fruits like Japanese pears, mangoes, mangosteens and even the humble starfruit can cost up to £1.50 each! A cup of coffee – this is a nation of tea drinkers and coffee is expensive – in a cafe might set you back £1 or more.

So you learn to live as the Brits do. Milk, flour, eggs and bread are cheap. So forget your traditional breakfast except for the occasional treat and opt for typical English fare which is relatively cheap and easy to throw together.

It's all mental assimilation and you'll come to grips with the cost of living here in time as long as you don't fight it with constant conversion.

Opening a Bank Account

This is a simple matter and does not entail much searching as Britain has banks on every high street; the four main ones are Barclays, NatWest (National Westminster), Lloyds and the Midland Bank. Chances are there is a branch near where you live or work.

London has as many international and commercial banks as any major city, and other British cities will have branches of at least Scottish, French, German and other major European banks. Given that you use banks during working hours, it is sensible to open an account where you can get to quickly. More and more banks are now opening on Saturday between 9.30 a.m. and 12 noon.

For a current or cheque account, you need a permanent fixed address, which you can prove either with a bill of sale or driving licence, and a letter from your employer or another bank which endorses your financial credibility.

For a deposit account, you don't need any guarantor or fixed address. Every bank has an information section where leaflets of every type of banking service are available.

Building Societies

The original concept of building societies, as the name fully implies, was to help people buy their own homes. Over the years they have moved even closer to becoming full-fledged banks where you can save, deposit, withdraw – in fact utilise pretty similar services that banks offer. As yet, building societies do not issue cheque books but offer instead a pass book which allows you to pay money into your account or to draw money out. For payments to a third party, you have to ask the building society to write a cheque as required – rather more time-consuming than a bank account. Major societies have branch offices all over Britain and it's a simple matter to withdraw money. A few have moved into the cash machine business and the banks are getting a bit queasy about this. They also have a few plus points to offset the lack of full banking facilities.

157

Unlike banks, building societies open from 9 to 5, and some on Saturdays. Most societies offer marginally better interest rates in their range of accounts and anything up to 9% gross. With tax deducted at source, a savings of £100,000 will yield £6000 or more a year, net.

When it comes to buying a house, you can leave it entirely to your building society to arrange the financing. My building society arranged everything when I bought and sold my first flat and later my present house. When you first approach a building society to arrange a mortgage, you might find some will insist on a minimum residential period of two years before they lend you any money.

I went to one leading society recommended by a friend, but they turned me down flat. It wasn't enough that I had a sizable bank draft waiting to be deposited. Their minimum residence period rule was inviolate. I subsequently went to the Leeds Building Society and they have been a good friend ever since – even making a sizable loan when I needed it.

The leading societies are the Halifax and the Abbey National, with a sprinkling of other smaller provincial ones. Shop around and go for one with a good track record or on recommendation. Operate a banking account by all means for day-to-day transactions, but keep your extra pennies in a building society to earn interest.

DIY

With cost of labour and non-existent weekend service, the acronym DIY makes for a hardboard jungle few can live without. Quite simply, Do-It-Yourself is far from a weekend activity for hobbyists.

It saves you a lot of money, never mind that the shelf you just fixed is less than perfectly horizontal. You can stand back and admire your prowess and be smug about not paying twice as much for a ready-made item even if your home is littered with DIY semi- and total disasters. One knock-together shelving unit I bought even came with a boldly printed instruction to 'first calm yourself and totally absorb the instructions' before fitting tongue to groove.

On weekends, DIY stores all over Britain – and some are the size of a football field – resemble ant-filled colonies with families, young couples and serious-looking hobbyists piling their trolleys with wash basins, paint, wrenches, coils of wire and everything you cannot do without in a home. Like domestic entrails. In the vast hangars of MFI, Payless, Texas and others are all you can buy to build a complete home from.

For most, it's a serious and practical matter of putting up fittings, repainting brick work, paving the garden path and the dozen and one things that need fixing in the home. It's almost impossible to get someone to do a one-off job, like wiring for your doorbell. Even if you can, the labour charges would drive you straight to the

nearest MFI. I once rang for a plumber to fix my washing machine which had clogged up. He came, reached into the underbelly of the machine, pulled out a soggy sock and pronounced my appliance in perfect working order again. It cost me £28 call-out fee plus an hour's (or part thereof) labour fee of £8.

Had I bothered to tinker around I could have done the same at no cost. It happened a second time and I was wise, and richer by £36.

Of course the *Yellow Pages* list any number of emergency services on 24-hour call. In practice, you rarely get anyone after 5 p.m. or on weekends. When your roof leaks after a violent hurricane, it will likely have to stay leaking till the following Monday. And then it might cost you some £80 for someone to lay on a bit of bitumen which you can self-help for perhaps one tenth the cost.

Few of us are naturally inclined towards messy plumbing and electrical wiring jobs, but, unless you are flush with cash, DIY is at least a saviour. You learn, with an ever-growing shed of tools, to fix this and that as they wear and tear. One major contributing factor in many homes is the shoddiness of fixtures to begin with.

Before homes are put on the market, the vendor will hastily and cheaply get things ship-shape the better to seduce buyers with. More than likeky, the owner would have gone out on a DIY binge and your would-be home is a glistening, gleaming and beeswaxed chocolate box – on the surface. Be wary of what you buy for many a thingamajig from DIY places look pretty but are far from durable.

Of course there are quality products but the mass market is generally of a uniform mediocrity. You could go to a bathroom specialist and fork out £1000 for a Victorian enamel affair with clawed legs or you could get a PVC one at Payless for £150. The difference being the former comes with professional installation and the latter? Well, DIY. Or at least a moonlighting plumber who, likely as not, will site it so that when you sit down in it, the floorboards creak.

When I got tired of my scruffy garden, I rang a professional garden-landscaper for an appraisal to redesign the unkempt patch. He wanted £300 not including cost of materials. All it needed was returfing and raising a few flowerbeds with brick work. When I finally found the courage to DIY, it cost me all of £50 including materials. Alright, the turf looks like a mole's battleground and the raised beds are less than perfectly aligned. In time, the hedgerows and ground cover plants will hide the multitude of sins but it was an enormous savings albeit for a garden that will definitely not win a Better Homes competition. It did represent five weekends of back-breaking labour hoisting 25lb bags of cement and making endless trips to ferry 120 bricks from MFI to car to home to garden.

If you are setting up home, be advised to invest in a set of basic tools to hammer, drill, plane and otherwise batten down carpets and banisters that tend to wrinkle and creak if not done professionally to begin with. An electric power drill is indispensable as most homes have brick walls that resist even unbending masonry nails.

With Britain's varying climate, every home has to withstand the stress that extremes of heat and cold can cause. A door isn't just a door if it's an old one. You need something called a draught ex-cluder, strips of synthetic around the frame to cut out chilly blasts. Even a half an inch (one centimetre) crack can chill your front hall within minutes.

Sealants around the bath tub often dry up, pop out and water seeps down the side to collect until damp rot sets in. Steam from hot water can do the most dastardly things in your bathroom. That beautiful regency striped washable wallpaper begins to peel if your DIY wasn't up to scratch. Mirrors scum over, lime scales every faucet because much of Britain's water is hard, and carpets need to be steam-cleaned every so often.

It will probably take a few months or even a year before you recover from the shock of frequent domestic fraying. Make DIY a top priority. You won't be sorry, out of pocket or neurotic trying to get service for jobs you can learn to do yourself. I never realised how indolent I was until settling here. I do now because it cost me half a week's wages just to rectify a fault in my washing machine. When your machine stops for no reason, think sock or be socked with an outrageous fee of anything up to £30 just for a call-out fee. For every appliance, make sure you take out a five-year mainte-nance packet which costs a fraction of what you might have to pay when something goes wrong.

Quite apart from the practical and money-saving considerations, DIY is absorbing, fun and therapeutic. You get a bashed thumb or two in the bargain, but as my knock-down shelf instructions read: 'Calm yourself first' and you soon get the hang of it.

There are things you never knew you had to do until you see your neighbour doing them. Like applying creosote to your garden picket fence. Creosote? It's a weather-proofing liquid that you coat

wood with so it resists rot and all the punishments of weather.

And DIY is not just buying packs that come together with instructions. It means keeping a close check on wear and tear that does not become blights in a house. Think of the problem when you decide to leave and have to sell it. Surveyors examine every house with a fine tooth comb and, unless it's in 'good nick', you'll find it may take months or even years before you can find a buyer.

In winter, water pipes can freeze solid if they are not properly insulated or 'lagged', or if your central heating system is not maintained properly. This is a professional twice-a-year job but you should check that the heating cycle does not allow circulating water to freeze during a cold snap. It got so cold one year that the fountains in Hyde Park froze in mid-spray!

If at the onset your tool kit is less than efficient, get neighbourly help. Most British homes have basic tools – even little old ladies know how to unwrench a stuck tap. It can take a lot of money to shock you out of a state of helplessness. It's money down the drain, but much less if you think DIY.

MEDICINE

The British National Health Service has never been an ideal and it frequently comes under fire for all sorts of reasons. Like the national welfare – social security – system, it has its shortcomings but in terms of the latest advances in medicine, Britain often leads the field. Don't forget this is a country of cradle-to-grave welfare and the strain on resources is usually stretched to the limit.

So much depends on who your doctor is, the area you live in – ratio of doctors to population – and the nature of your illness. Coming from any country where state health services are efficient and private medical treatment relatively inexpensive, Britain's state of health can be a rude shock.

When you first settle in, find a doctor near your house and register every member of the household. Once registered, you have

You do not need a doctor's prescription for medicines to treat common ailments, such as colds and coughs. The local chemist will advise you on what to take for simple ailments.

to see the same doctor if he or she is available. Surgery hours (the common term for clinics' operating hours) are usually between 10 a.m. and 12 noon, and 5 and 6 p.m., Monday to Friday. Usually the clinic is closed one day every week. Every visit has to be by appointment and doctors don't take kindly to treating minor ailments like coughs and colds.

Self-medication is the norm for these sniffles, with chemist chains all over the country. You visit a doctor for more severe symptoms or when they persist despite self-medication. Between surgery hours, it's difficult to get a doctor and all you can do is to leave a message on the answering service. Only in an emergency will your doctor see you on weekends.

Many doctors do their rounds in hospitals in between their surgery hours and are not at your beck and call. In an extreme emergency, ring the hospital near you, but admittance will depend on the severity of the ailment and how busy they are. Admittance to an NHS hospital is almost always via a doctor's referral. Hospitals are usually busy, so be prepared to wait until a doctor can see you unless you're very bad. Hospitals in the major cities are generally understaffed and bed space is on a priority basis.

All treatment is free under national health and you pay for the prescription if you're over 18. Both treatment and prescription are free for under 16s and up to 18 if you are in full-time study. Depending on the prescription, medicines are generally under £5.

Clinics do not dispense medicine – all prescriptions have to be taken to the nearest chemist. The system is fairly rigid and you simply have to abide by it. Not all doctors will give you a thorough examination – mine just sits and listens to the symptoms and prescribes accordingly. Remember some doctors in heavily populated boroughs may have as many as several thousand patients under their care and they simply do not have the time for protracted individual examination, unless your symptoms demand it.

Generally your doctor will listen to your chest and check your throat. You get all of five minutes if you're lucky. This is not painting a dismal picture of the medical services. The majority of patients suffer from ailments that really can be treated with patent medicines from the local chemist. Every chemist has one or several fully qualified pharmacists who will give you all the help you need, short of an examination.

You soon realise it's much more convenient to self-medicate, though you may pay marginally more without a prescription, unless you are sure you need antibiotics, which are only available by prescription.

The biggest problem with the National Health Service is surgery. Unless it's a dire emergency, you may have to wait months, even years, to have a minor surgery done. Like removing tonsils. This is compounded by a shortage of government doctors. The reasons are two-fold. Salaries are low and hours are long. You often read stories of housemen in government hospitals doing straight 90-hour shifts with scarcely any break.

Those who can afford it prefer to go into private practice, which earns them much more money, and they work more regular hours. As for house calls during off surgery hours, at night and on weekends under national health, you may as well forget it. Unless you're old, infirm and have had a bad accident, and your doctor is concerned enough to see you straightaway. Otherwise calling for an ambulance is the best option.

Private medicine is very expensive and not necessarily more efficient. It all depends on your relationship with your family doctor, whether he takes calls or is permanently unavailable after hours.

There are all kinds of private medical insurance policies you can buy if you should worry about urgent treatment for chronic ailments like heart problems and old age symptoms.

Hospital visiting hours are generally flexible, but the ratio of staff to patients is chronically imbalanced. British hospitals do not pamper patients, and nurses, also chronically overworked, get stroppy if you are excessively demanding. But once under hospital care, you get proper medical treatment.

The pharmaceutical business in Britain is a huge enterprise because most people self-medicate and avoid seeing the doctor unless it is absolutely necessary. More often than not, dragging yourself out of bed to make an appointment and then having to wait interminably can make you more ill. Send someone out to the chemist giving the pharmacist your symptoms and you generally get better without all the hassle.

Getting an appointment to see a specialist is another long-winded affair. Most specialists will not make a telephone appointment. They need a letter from your GP and then it may take weeks before they can slot you in. In a country where you are likely to live a few miles from the nearest doctor, clinic or hospital, keeping a medicine chest of basic drugs is the most sensible remedial action. You could die of frustration just getting an appointment.

If you think you have something contagious, don't just march into your doctor's clinic without telephoning. Many doctors use their own home as clinic and may have children around – like our doctor. When my son had glandular fever, she was adamant about him not seeing her and made arrangements for him to be sent to hospital.

Dental Treatment

Basically the same as medical treatment, but less of a hassle as dental surgeons do not have as many patients as GPs. All students under 18 get free treatment – even expensive braces should you need them. Adults pay 75%, the other 25% comes under NHS.

Opticians

National Health covers only for under 18s and even then with a limited range of frames which are all pretty awful and uniformly un-attractive. Private prescriptions for glasses are expensive and an average pair costs upwards of £50 – as much as £300 for designer frames. Shop around as choice of frames is cosmetic anyway.

Hay Fever

A peculiar problem hits millions every year on the onset of summer. It's caused by the level of pollen in the air and, when you get it badly, your eyes itch and stream and you feel fluish for weeks. Like the common cold, it defies medication and can affect anybody. Weather reports in summer give pollen counts everyday so that you know how to at least avoid coming into contact with it by staying indoors.

Winter Chills

Adapting to the cold is one of the most common complaints among foreigners from warmer climates. With the first blast of wintry wind, your resistance to colds is lowered considerably and even a little draught from under the door can cause sniffles. There are dozens of cold cures available but it depends on the severity. Massive doses of vitamin C are the best prevention I find.

Cold Rashes

The first time I had these I thought I had shingles. You get uncontrollable itches all over for no reason and the best cure is to soak in a hot bath with some medicated bath salts.

Arthritis

Peculiar to cold climates, this is a debilitating disease that often cripples people badly. It generally affects people in their 60s but is not uncommon among younger people. Treatment is difficult and often ineffective. Improper heating in the home compounds this.

– Chapter Eight –

EDUCATION

SCHOOL AND SKOOL

Education policies in Britain in the past were fairly flexible. Most schools could set their own curriculum, time tables and methodology, albeit under supervision of one of the 104 Local Education Authorities. However, the 1988 Education Act set up a National Curriculum which went into practice in September 1989. By law all state-run schools have applied the curriculum since 1989.

What it is in simple terms, for those who have school-age children, is a prescribed syllabus of nine subjects for primary schools: Art, English, Geography, History, Mathematics, Music, Physical Education, Science and Technology/Design. For secondary schools, a 10th subject (a modern foreign language) is added.

There have been heated arguments for and against this. Britain is one of the few countries in Europe which did not have a national curriculum and supporters felt it was about time. Their argument was sound – children who change schools would not have to suffer the trauma of curriculum change.

The introduction of a modern foreign language as an entitlement was seen as a positive step away from hide-bound and often whimsical decisions by school heads to teach or not to teach a foreign language. Until now, French has been dominant. Yet, six out of 10 end up knowing next to nothing. Most drop French at 13 or 14 years of age. English is so widely spoken in other countries that there has been little compunction to learn even the rudiments of a foreign language. Many British, though, harbour more than a little envy of people who speak more than one language.

It is expected that European languages will dominate. Then again, it could be Russian, Urdu, Gujerati or any one of the Asian languages spoken by Britain's ethnic groups. What is significant is the British Government's decision not to take part in the European 'Lingua' programme. This would have required all member states to offer two EC languages in their schools. For the moment, most British baulk at having to study even one!

The syllabi called 'Attainment Targets' have 10 levels in each subject covering the 11 years of compulsory education from age five to 16. Highest levels will fuse in the GCSE – General Certificate of Secondary Education.

Primary school students from now will have to grapple with the mechanics of high tech. Parents fear their children will be highly stressed from all this. What happened to Nature Study? All that healthy rambling among flora and fauna should be preserved.

For the moment it's too premature to assess how this will affect students in the long term. But the previous systems obviously had too many flaws and many British children who learnt their 3Rs under the comprehensive system could not even spell simple words.

It has been a standing joke among the British themselves. Regional dialects only compounded the confusion among younger children who were taught to pronounce a word one way only to hear it in a totally strange guise at home.

CHOICE OF SCHOOLS

What concerns you if you have school-going children is more immediate. Which school? State or private (fee-paying)? Are there other ethnic children? Will he or she adapt? When we arrived, our son was 11 and at the most crucial stage of his education. We asked all these questions, checked with dozens of schools and the education authorities.

At the end of the day, there was one major consideration that tended to overrule the others. The school's proximity to home. Of course you could do it the other way by finding a school first and then deciding to buy or rent accommodation. Except that your choice of home is equally important and sublimating it to choice of school could be a disservice to your whole family. Once you have decided, it is a simple matter of enrolling with the school before the start of each school year in September. Obviously, the earlier you register, the better chances you have of securing a place.

The other problem was the option of private schools – paradoxically called 'public' in Britain – that offered quality education. There are thousands of schools in Britain, both state and public. There are bad public schools just as there are good state schools. But a fee-paying public school has the autonomy to structure its education policies with a much freer hand. Most are well-funded and facilities are less likely to be stretched as in state schools.

By the same token of numbers and facilities, state school students can expect a more raucous time in most extra curricular activities. A foreign student in a big school with a small ethnic population may feel a greater sense of isolation. How he mingles, makes friends and establishes himself is largely dependent upon himself.

Of course there will be the odd bully, bigot or nuisance element. There is no ready answer to this problem. Only personal grit and determination not to be intimidated.

My son's primary public school – called a prep school – only had 10 or 11 pupils in a class. Compare this with some 30-40 in a state primary school. Of course there was more individual attention, and most of the students come from fairly middle class homes. What is fundamental is that parents want the best for their children, within the boundaries of their financial capabilities. And assiduous checking will help you determine which school you like best.

The student population in many schools is also a worry. Up to a thousand is common in a comprehensive compared with several hundred, or much less, in a fee-paying school. If you decide to send your children to a public school, be prepared for fees anywhere between £500 and £1500 per term, for day school.

ENGLISH AS SHE IS SPOKE

The teaching of English is a matter on which many hold strong views. Schools have a clear responsibility to teach Standard English but teachers have a difficult problem. They cannot denigrate non-standard regional dialects which rules out elocution lessons to produce, if not uniformity, at least clear, well-enunciated English. There has been much groundswell feeling for Britain's regional accents, a return to salt-of-the-earth accents and slang that are now a feature of the hitherto sacrosanct BBC. The argument that language is dynamic must stand and what is important is the meaning conveyed, rather than what is the (arguable) norm. In this sense, it's an invaluable education to pick up on regional accents and even hone one's ability to practise them.

If you have the ability to switch from Standard English to whatever ethnic or regional form (e.g. Italian lilt or cockney) without the attendant derisory mockery, then it's a plus. Adapting this facility to a slightly different set of phonetics would seem a breeze.

UNIFORMS AND OTHER COSTS

On the practical side, putting children through school in Britain has its normal problems. Almost every school has a uniform, for both boys and girls. This is usually a blazer and trousers or skirt. Most state schools will recommend their clothiers – usually some high street chain. If the blazer is a basic blue, grey or black, you have little problem with a growing youngster who may go through several a year!

If the school is private, chances are it will have a blazer that is unique – like purple and black stripes that only one shop provides. Now whether this is engineered with commercial profit in mind, I cannot say. What I can say is that, if they run out of stock size, you're in trouble. Blazers are also expensive as they are well-made, lined and much like a man's jacket.

Then you have to worry about the accessories like scarves (again

All schools have a uniform, usually in a neutral colour which is quite easy to buy new or even second hand.

in the school colours), rugby shirts, football shorts, shoes, cricket whites, rowing gear, fencing equipment ad infinitum, depending on your children's sporting inclinations and the school's facilities.

If you can afford a public school education, you will benefit from their emphasis on a wide range of activities for their pupils. At a rough estimate, expect to spend between £300-£500 the initial year over and above fees for primary public school and anything up to £800 for secondary school extra curricular activities. Depending on the growth rate of your child, you might get away with much less cost the following years.

State school equipment is all funded by the local councils and in any case emphasis on sports like fencing, rowing and cricket gets low priority. Given the student population in most state schools, fielding a team for any sport is much less a problem and therefore, the pressure on the individual to be gung ho sporty is lighter.

The difference in the two systems really boils down to the ratio of teachers to pupils. What results is really dependent on the quality of teachers and input level of pupils. And behind it all is parental guidance and encouragement, be it character development or academic prowess through academic or physical activity.

The teacher to pupil ratios and academic achievements at the state or comprehensive schools vary enormously. You can only send your child to the school in the 'catchment area' you live in: many families do in fact move house in order to give their children the benefit of a better state school. In suburban areas and small towns in the provinces, little fault will be found with either the academic or extra curricular syllabus taught at state schools.

All secondary schools and those primary schools with over 300 pupils are now allowed to 'opt out' of local education authority control and become grant-maintained schools funded directly from central government. All parents have the chance to vote in a ballot to do this, though the final decision is in the hands of the Secretary of State for education. Along with the National Curriculum, this is part of the 1988 Education Reform Act, which is geared to make schools and school governors more responsible for school financing, and also to give parents a greater role in education.

Teachers in Britain do not enjoy any particular status, and state salaries are low, which has led to shortages as many graduates turn away from the teaching profession. There have been lengthy teachers strikes – one in 1989-90 severely disrupted the schooling of state pupils for an entire year – caused both by low salaries and by antagonism against the Conservative government's low spending on education. The introduction of the National Curriculum also meant considerable unpaid additional preparation work for all teachers, as syllabi were only confirmed shortly before implementation.

SCHOOL DINNERS

The British version of tuck shop sustenance, at the best of times, is hardly haute cuisine. There has been much flak directed at many schools, or rather their local authorities, for serving rubbish or at best, tasteless, if nutritious, food. And with more and more ethnic mix, catering can be a nightmare when 800 students with widely different tastes sit down to lunch. British school hours are mostly between 9 and 3 or 4 p.m., so lunch is a legitimate period.

You can't expect gourmet cooking under the circumstances. Given that British cooking is known for its unventuresome blandness, school meals have become the target of much self-effacing British humour.

Public schools discourage the bringing of your own food for various reasons, the chief being that it will single out your child as being spoilt and soft. Also your fees include lunch and all refreshments, so why throw away good money? State schools are more liberal on the matter and it's entirely up to the individual whether he or she wants to pack sandwiches or sit down to school meals – though for those from very poor families, the school dinner, however bland, is the most wholesome meal they get all day.

BOARDING SCHOOLS

Boarding is a choice dictated by several reasons. You may want a particular school at all costs but it's too far away for day attendance. Generally, those British parents who send their children to boarding school do so, so that they learn self-sufficiency, independence and other spartan values that are considered to be good for character development. It is also expensive, with some top boarding places charging up to £10,000 a year.

All in all, boarding school can be prohibitive with investment not always justifying quality of education. There have been a few stories of boarders taking drugs and getting thrown out with parents wringing their hands at such a waste of money.

SECURITY AND SAFETY

With Britain's seasons, journeys to and from school can be fraught with dangers from the elements as well as criminal intent, especially for younger children. Not all schools, state or public, can provide transport and even then, pickup points are not always convenient.

The fundamental has to be parental care in accompanying younger children, even for a short distance. In winter, when it gets dark by 5 p.m., this is particularly important. Snow, ice, blizzards and fog are all potential dangers, and proper clothing is important.

It is best, if you can, to find out if other children living nearby are going the same way. Arrange for them to keep each other company for there is no better deterrent to evil intent than groups.

Where dangers lie in the school itself, possibly from bad hats and bullies, the only recourse is to switch schools or make effective reports to the school head. Unfortunately, if you send a child to a school with hundreds of pupils, this can be a tricky problem.

The problems in this quarter would have been more or less eliminated during your choice of school. The most important is to talk to the school head, ask to be shown around and look at every-thing before you decide. Talk to friends who have children in those schools, ask the children themselves about conditions, whether they encounter racism, prejudice, etc.

RACISM

Even the most innocent of infantile ribbing can be misconstrued as racism. Of course it can happen in any institution where there is a mix of nationalities. It's not an easy problem to eradicate, only that parents should not overreact to complaints of such schoolboy jibing.

You can only hope that your children's schoolmates have been brought up with values that proscribe prejudice against colour, race and creed. If there are racist taunts directed at your children because of rubbed-off values from unenlightened parents or individual bigotry, the best way is to speak to the headmaster and determine the

At school, your child will make friends with children of various races.

EDUCATION

seriousness of the problem. Of late, reverse bigotry has been making front page news. The pernicious 'special needs' doctrine of the 1976 Race Relations Act has turned the minds of many Asian Indian parents. At the Springfield Junior School in Birmingham where only 12 of the 600 students are of ethnic origin, an English schoolteacher was sacked for not speaking Urdu!

Many of the parents have not learned English despite being in England for more than a dozen years. There obviously has not been the integration necessary for them to assimilate and learn enough English to have useful parent-teacher relationships. The English-speaking Asian parents are vociferous in their objection to such an attitude, but the seeds of the problem have been too deeply sown. They are aghast that many in their community have not learnt even rudimentary English and, worse, actually resist learning.

Boroughs with high ethnic population have been pushing hard on anti-racist education that often goes over the brink of sensibility.

Educationists have hit out at this as intellectual nonsense knowing that some half a million ethnic immigrants, perhaps much more, are functionally illiterate in English. In this light, accusations that Britain is a racist society seem grossly out of step.

In defence of the National Curriculum, it would appear that an overbalance of ethnic language and cultural education threatens to undermine the status of English. They are after all living in an English country. And with something like 150 different languages spoken, such race lobbies can only upset the delicate balance of an educational system. Not to mention the enormous cost if public affairs are to be conducted in different languages. The question of bi-lingual schools has so far not been mentioned by the education authorities, the argument above negating this step.

Whatever turn it takes, racism is a sensitive issue and rightly or wrongly, decision makers are naturally chary of taking remedial action. One good point made was that many ethnic children are already saturated in their own culture 18 out of 24 hours. What is the rationale of urging their school to celebrate such culture when they are there essentially to be educated in English and ultimately to become British citizens in the fullest sense?

My feeling is there is enormous goodwill and tolerance in this country, blighted occasionally by the outbursts of racial bigots who see themselves as victims, fuelled by race lobbies. In this sense, the Chinese are different in that they spend almost all their time working hard and carving their fortunes. Hardly any of them are involved in race lobbies and they prefer to steer clear of any racial arguments. It is also significant that many second and third generation Chinese speak perfect English, accents and all, and yet are fully conversant in their native tongues. Even if they are not, their parents are generally not bothered, if at all in a resigned way. As for Chinese not being part of the curriculum, their solution was to organise Mandarin and Cantonese classes through their community associations.

THE AGES

Most parents would like their children to go to a kindergarten by the time they are four or five, even play school at three, but this is more out of expediency than necessity. By law, all children must be educated between the ages of five and 16. By the age of 16, they will have sat for their GCSE exams and, if results and personal inclinations dictate, will move on to two years of A-levels. By the end of their first year of A-levels, most students will have narrowed down their choice of subjects and opted for the university they want.

Generally, it is advisable to apply a year in advance to ensure you get a place, pending results. Entrance requirements depend on type of course, standard of university and where it is. All university students (British citizens and permanent residents) qualify for a student grant that pays fees and subsistence. Whether the average £2600 per year is sufficient depends on the individual. Parents are asked to contribute, depending on their means, to their children's subsistence, though tuition fees are generally covered by the local

179

authority grants. A scheme for student loans, similar to the one in the USA, is currently being mooted, but it is extremely controversial. Those students considering a career in the armed forces can sign up for a certain time – generally five years or more – in return for the army, navy or RAF paying some or all of their fees.

First year students live in hostel but do not need to after one year. The accommodation problem is currently acute and some university students have to bunk on floors and share cramped quarters in some of the more popular universities. For second year students, especially in London, finding accommodation to suit their budget of roughly £50 a week is difficult. There is a continuous moan that the grant is insufficient and rented accommodation is in short supply in most urban areas. Hostel accommodation is at best adequate, in some cases depressing, but nothing that a few cheerful posters and loving comforts from home cannot uplift.

State Schools

Most schools are entirely the responsibility of an LEA (Local Education Authority). They are known as state schools. In addition there are voluntary schools, often founded by a religious body, e.g. the Church of England, which are generally free, though some may have minimal fees.

Choices

Some secondary schools and very few primary schools admit boys or girls only. Most secondary schools are comprehensive, i.e. they admit pupils of all abilities. Grammar and secondary modern schools may admit according to specific ability.

Transport

The LEA may help with fares or provide transport if the school is more than 3 miles (4.8 kilometres) from your home or 2 miles (3.2 kilometres) for children under 8.

Priority

Very popular schools often get more applications than they have places. Usually priority is given to children living locally, or who have siblings in the school. Religious foundation schools may give priority to practising members of the faith.

These apply only when a school has more applicants than places or when it has not reached its published admissions limit.

Special Educational Needs (SEN)

LEAs must place a child in an ordinary school if the parents want it, and the school can provide proper facilities. If the child's needs are so great that he needs special help, your LEA will help with the appropriate advice on choice of special schools. Some schools in most areas have a special unit for SEN children.

Meals

All students pay for their lunches at an average cost of 50p for a substantial meal. Milk is not free but fairly inexpensive.

GCSE

The General Certificate of Secondary Education (GCSE) has replaced O-levels and CSE (Certificate of Secondary Education). It is awarded at the end of a two-year course based on assessment as well as end-of-term exams generally at age 15 or 16.

What is TVEI?

Technical and Vocational Education Initiative is not a qualification or an exam. It is a new approach to learning for 14-18 year olds. Schools and colleges are given more money to make lessons more practical and relevant to adult life and work. Some schools are already offering this. Check with your LEA.

CPVE

Certificate of Pre-Vocational Education is for 16 year olds who have not decided on a career yet. A one-year course, it offers a chance to gain skills and work experience in a range of job areas.

YTS

Youth Training Scheme is for 16 year olds who want to leave full-time education and training. It is a two-year programme which offers a chance to experience different types of work in a workplace.

Useful Addresses

Department of Education and Science
Publications Despatch Centre
Government Building
Honeypot Lane
Stanmore
Middlesex HA7 1AZ

The CPVE Unit
46, Britannia Street
London WC1X 9RG
Tel: 071 278 2468

Pre-school Playgroups Association (PPA)
61-63 Kings Cross Road
London WC1X 9LL
Tel: 071 833 0991

LEARNING ENGLISH IN BRITAIN

Coming to Britain to learn English can be fun. But it can also be miserable, lonely and expensive if your English is rudimentary. Probably the best way is total immersion – that is, make friends with the locals and take it from there. Living here makes it imperative that you not only need to be sufficiently proficient in the language but to understand the argot, colloquialism and quirky usage. Schools only teach the fundamental – the rest is up to the individual to absorb, apply and ultimately become totally conversant with the semantics of the language.

Contact the Association for Recognised English Language Teaching Establishments in Britain at 2, Pontypool Place, Valentine Place, London SE1 8QF, tel: 071 242 3136. They are recognised by the British Council, the official English language and cultural organisation. English language teaching is a huge money-making industry in Britain, especially London, so be aware that there are plenty of shady organisations. Just because it has an official sounding name and is a bona fide college does not mean you will get your money's worth. Go by personal recommendation or check with the official listings published by the above organisation.

There are literally thousands of English language schools throughout Britain with different facilities, for instance, residential, English for executives, adult vacation courses, junior vacation courses, etc.

INDEPENDENT FEE-PAYING SCHOOLS

The Independent Schools Information Service (ISIS) has eight regional centres in Britain and Ireland and a national HQ in London.

There are 2500 schools in Britain, independent of local or central government, sometimes called fee-paying schools or private schools. The latter term is not strictly accurate, for most of these schools are not run for private profit. Most have their own board of governors who make sure surplus income is put back into running costs. The head is responsible to the governors but is usually given a free hand to choose staff and make day-to-day decisions. 75% of private school students leave with 5 or more GCSEs. More than 50% leave with two or more A-levels. More than 25% of university students are from independent schools although only 7% of all children attend independent schools in Britain.

183

Religious Faiths

There are independent schools for Catholics, Methodists, Quakers and Jews, with many having links with the Church of England.

The Ages and Types

2 to 19: All through school
2 to 7: Pre-prep, Nursery or Kindergarten
7 to 11-plus or 13-plus: Junior Schools or Prep Schools
11 to 18: Senior Schools or Secondary Schools
13 to 18: Senior Schools
16-plus: Sixth Form

When to Register Your Child

At least a year or even two in advance, if the school is popular, particularly day schools in London and other cities.

The Headmaster

A good head makes the school just as a poor one can break it. A good head is one who is more concerned about the welfare of his wards than trying to impress you with the handsomeness and history of his school premises.

Addresses

ISIS International
56, Buckingham Gate
London SW1E 6AG
Tel: 071 630 8790

ISIS Regions
Central England:
Woodstock, Oxon OX7 1YF
Tel: (0993) 813 006

Eastern England:
Church Farm
Saxlington
Holt, Norfolk NR25 7JY
Tel: (0328) 830 595

London and Southeast England:
Murray House
3, Vandon Street
London SW1H 0AN
Tel: (071) 222 7274

Northern England and North Wales:
Mearbeck Farmhouse
Twaite Lane
Tatham
Lancaster, Lancs. LA2 8PR

South and Mid-Wales:
The Hollies
Rectory Drive
St Athan
Barry, S. Glam. CF6 9PD
Tel: (0446) 750 120

Scotland:
Headfort School
Kells Co Meath
Tel: (048) 40065

Chapter Nine

LEISURE ACTIVITIES

MEDIA
Newspapers

For anyone enamoured of the printed word, Britain is a wordsmith's paradise. Whatever your tastes, whether you are an egghead or voyeur, high-brow or inclined to sex and sensationalism, there's a broadsheet or tabloid for you. Your first encounter with Britain's popular press – often given the ignominious slag-off as 'gutter press' – is likely to be startling to say the least. At first glance the *Sunday Sport* might seem to be all about football scores and cricket overs. Perhaps a few pages; the rest are devoted to coverage of events quite out of this world.

"Woman gives birth to alien!"

"Elvis spotted shopping in Burbank!"

The headlines scream, enticing you to pore over the features therein that are the antithesis of responsible journalism. Pictorial coverage has nothing to do with good or bad taste, simply overt sensationalism. Nothing is sacrosanct – not even the physically handicapped. It's not a newspaper – it's a window on the weird, unbelievable, a veritable sci-fi serving that purports to make sense of the ridiculous.

Or if other people's sex lives and assorted skeletons in cupboards make your Sunday reading, you'd devour the *News of the World* with relish. Everyone in the public eye is fair game, be it getting out of a car in mini-skirt or canoodling in a night club. Nothing and nobody is sacrosanct – not even the spectre of libel suits – to this rag mag. Its reportage has landed the paper in the law courts but it goes on selling by the millions. No celebrity in Britain is safe from this paper if he is less than discreet or prudent. Or if the truth is less than interesting, thinly-veiled aspersions of sexual perversion and everything deviant make up the copy.

Of course these papers outsell such respectable journalistic flagships as *The Times*, *The Guardian* and *The Independent*. It depends on whether you want a lascivious bite out of the gossip grapevine or to ponder over serious political dissertations. Sunday reading in Britain can take all of your day, even if your tastes are singularly pristine; a whole weekend if prurient and eclectic. Each Sunday paper is thick enough to make a door wedge, plus the assorted colour magazines and supplements. They seek to inform, provoke, entertain, titillate and tantalise. And they do, to the exclusion of all other activities.

Some get right under your skin. *The Independent*'s hoarding advertisements snidely question your individualism: "Are you independent enough to share our views?" Others sell on the basis of pull-no-punches reportage. One says there are no sacred cows within its pages. The problem arises when a *Sun* – the one with the page three nude – reader does not know the meaning of this symbolic animal. Is it a farming journal then?

The paper you read, of course, reflects your level of intellect. It doesn't matter if you buy *The Times* to wrap fish and chips with it – reading it on the tube gives you a certain status. Like the filofax, serious broadsheets rustle up an aura for those diffident about reading *The Sun* in public. It can get disconcerting when half a dozen pairs of eyes are boring into you while yours burn into the naked body of the page three girl. This is the raison d'être of *The Sun*. Once you've had your fill of the nymph in all her fleshy flaunt, the rest of the paper is made up of juicy bits of news hardly likely to shake the world. A few page three girls have gone on to make fortunes from their physical endowments. Such is media exposure.

If you want to know about people – pop stars and glitterati to be more specific – read *The People*.

Somewhere between these two opposite poles are *The Mirror*, *Express*, *Today* and *Daily Mail* that are basically serious tabloids but not serious enough to tax the brain cells. The news and intellectual views do not necessarily sell newspapers. A situation that has Britain's educationists wringing their hands in despair. What can be going wrong with a country that sells millions of a paper with little else to offer apart from naked bosoms and mere thousands of a heavyweight, thinking man's newssheet like *The Times*?

Opinions will vary on this disparity but the tycoons of trashy media go on laughing all the way to the bank. And if circulation appears to be dropping, why there's always the giveaways, lotto games and hard cold cash to boost sales.

London's only evening newspaper, *The Standard*, is a hodge-podge of both serious and frivolous. As a monopoly, the captive market keeps it afloat. Others have tried and folded because newspaper loyalty is an inexplicable poser in Britain.

As a nation of commuters and Sunday domestic plodders, a 10-

minute skim on the tube, even a protracted read on the train and weekend flipping over gossip and pictorial exposes win hands down over masses of grey text. With at least 20 national, 1500 provincial newspapers and dozens of other specialist and other general information publications, no taste is left out, however deviant. Every borough has its own newspaper, usually stuffed with advertisements for everything from aspirin to zoologists. These come free and are pushed through your mail box whether you read them or not. I find them useful to flog my used stuff, or to get hold of a second-hand heater. Most major newsagents in the big cities with cosmopolitan communities stock German, Italian, Spanish, French and Arabic national papers. Chinatown shops, even supermarkets in London, Birmingham, Manchester and other cities with any sizable Chinese population stock a number of Chinese language papers. And there is now a European paper as well.

Magazines

There must be more magazines on newsstands in Britain than dead leaves in autumn. The premier ones like *Woman*, *Woman's Own*, *House and Garden*, *Vogue* and the like have been selling for decades with scarcely any change in format. But the past decade has seen hitherto rock-solid magazine publishing houses reaching for the valium. Inflation, changing tastes, distribution costs and other factors can force a new magazine to go under within weeks of hitting the newsstands. And the established ones cannot afford to be complacent because of the competition. Magazines for blacks, for the handicapped, for the young, not-so-young, yuppie, executive, sports-mad, new woman, etc., entice with glossy covers. Most are within the £2 range and are very accessible. Every newsagent, makeshift stand outside train stations and supermarket sells them hot from the press.

DIY journals, home repairs, homeopathy: all the answers to the minutiae of life's daily trials are spelled out in reassuring tones.

Newsstands all over Britain present a cosmopolitan array of newspapers and magazines in English and other European languages.

Come Christmas, every other magazine will tell you how to stuff a turkey, plan your countdown to that grand family dinner and what to do with your chestnut shells. It's comforting to know that some publication somewhere will tell you how to make quince jam, unplug a clogged sink and mend your own dentures. Where service doesn't come cheap, if it comes at all, Britain's general interest and self-help magazines can be your lifeline to sanity. Among the chain stores which stock such magazines and have branches across Britain are names like W.H. Smith and John Menzies.

Television

The number of people in Britain who choose to ignore television is so small they never count in statistical studies. Given the influence of this most invasive of mass media, surveys concern themselves with how many sets each household has and how many hours people spend watching.

The accusatory fingers are out every so often that children are hopelessly addicted to TV. The latest survey shows that one in every four British children has his OWN TV set, and is glued to it for 13 hours a week, which works out to a solid two hours every evening. A cause for parental worry with many wringing their hands in despair that there is little control over what the kids watch, ruining their imagination in the process, never mind that homework takes a poor second place.

This is especially so when they go beyond the 9 p.m. watershed for adult programmes that show explicit sex, violence and other undesirable facets of low life. Others worry that television is a harbinger of family life breakdown. Socialists and mass media analysts' efforts to alert the public to television's pervasive dangers seem so much waffling. Now satellite TV has joined the circuit and homes all over Britain are sprouting dish antennae to add even more channels to the existing four.

The two channels, Sky and BSB (British Satellite Broadcasting), which recently merged, have spent millions enticing the public to bring even more package news, entertainment and sport into their living rooms. The public outcry is that the line between education/ information and negative influence is thin enough as it is without the world becoming the viewer's oyster. Watchdogs, watersheds and censorship aside, British television does indeed pervade, dis-tract, entertain and alarm, depending on your moral views, self-discipline and, in the case of parents, vetting powers.

BBC1 and BBC2 are non-commercial stations depending on annual licence fees and government subsidy. Carlton TV and Channel 4 have yet to bombard viewers with commercials between heartbeats as is the case with American television but do have enough 'breaks' to make watching irksome. Of the four channels, Carlton TV is the only 24-hour channel though no survey has yet been done about what the viewership figures are during the wee small hours. Security guards on night duty must find this a comforting distraction.

Except for BBC 2, the other channels vie ceaselessly for viewership from six in the morning, with snap, crackle and pop 'breakfast television' that can range from the inane to the arty. Contents are a hodgepodge of current affairs, world news and pop gossip that aim to capture the attention of millions of people rushing off to work before 9 a.m. The ratings war becomes the yardstick for the rise or fall of such programming and the efforts to sustain viewers often reach ridiculous heights. One breakfast session was suffering so badly that the producers decided to bring in a character called Roland Rat – a glove puppet. It didn't say much for viewers' cranial matter when the toothy rodent pulled the programme from the brink of cancellation to an all-time popularity!

Provincial stations like Central, TVS, Channel, TSW, Anglia and Yorkshire have somewhat different schedules but pool their news coverage on the independent Carlton TV and Channel 4 channels. All papers print daily viewing schedules for every station. It is as impossible to use a blanket description for British television as it is to pigeonhole public tastes. You could use every adjective in the book and still not encompass what appears on the little box. At best, accolades and brickbats are only a reflection of individual taste.

Commercials

No more, no less annoying than any other commercial station with an average of four 'ads' each break and three breaks in a half-hour programme. British commercials are in a class of their own, often more entertaining than the programme they interrupt and many commercial 'stars' are cult figures in their own right. A beautiful woman may be seen selling coffee one minute and the next, she's appearing in some situation comedy on another channel. Many actors and actresses between jobs grab at the lucrative contracts offered by manufacturers, which often catapult them to stardom that bit movie parts do not.

By the same token, many top stars are seen endorsing products and become identified so strongly with their product that the roles they play in straight dramas become so much less credible.

There are no commercials on the two BBC channels though there has been constant talk about the Beeb going commercial. So far, the world's most famous broadcasting name is resisting the lure of multi-million pound revenue with the argument that quality will be compromised if they sell their souls to consumerism.

Cigarette advertising is totally banned, and underwear and alcohol are strictly controlled by a code of time and suitability. The impression one gets is an overwhelming barrage of household products, almost always with a wry twist of humour in the message. This is a distinctive British feature. Hard-sell commercials are far outweighed by those that feature the inimitable British touch for humour. Whatever the product or service, the treatment is inevitably humorous and memorable. Britain, in fact, is regarded by the rest of the advertising world as the think tank of creativity. The world's largest and most successful agency is Saatchi and Saatchi in London which packaged Margaret Thatcher slickly enough to win her crucial votes.

Watching commercials is a marvellous way of boning up on British consumer goods without leaving the house. In a few months you'll learn the comparative merits of one lager against another, which bread is healthier, what your dog likes to eat (how they know I'll never know!), when and where to buy spring lamb, which car is tested by robots and driven by humans (it won an award), etc. In this sense, it is a matchless education for a foreigner getting to grips with the British lifestyle. After all, you don't want to use just any detergent – it's got to be the one that makes your whites cleaner than white. I say, do not disappear to make a cup of tea when the commercials are on. If nothing else, it's gloriously funny to see and hear chimpanzees extolling the virtues of PG Tips!

Documentaries

When the British produce good documentaries, they rarely have a peer. In the area of wildlife and ecology, the BBC has a stable of first-rate programmes that have not paled even after repeat showings over decades. Perhaps the most distinguished of all documentary creators is David Attenborough who has chronicled an immense range of subjects from bird's nest gathering in Borneo to the sex life of desert ants. A past master of wildlife minutiae, his programmes have rarely been off the air for the past 20 years, each one more beguiling, educational and entertaining than the previous one.

Other documentaries of the artistic, historical and entertainment genre are generally very watchable. In the field of art, British television provides an absorbing and often scintillating insight that museums can never hope to do. The weekly *Antiques Roadshow* attempts to play the role of dream merchant in identifying bric-à-brac brought along by hopeful owners. Viewers join in the excitement of a possible discovery that a dusty *objet d'art* might turn up to be a rare treasure worth a small fortune! The queue is unending and the programme looks like it will run and run. Watching it makes you want to rummage through your old chest in the hope of finding that your ginger jar is really a Ming vase.

History and theatrical arts do not get enough air time, alas; they are deemed elitist entertainment hardly likely to match the viewership of such glitz as *Dallas* and *Dynasty*. Which explains why most serious documentaries are aired late at night – past prime time. Ratings, you see, are the barometer of populist taste and programmes of any intellect tend to be slotted in when the masses are in bed. No survey has yet been made to find out if eggheads go to bed later.

Situation Comedies (Sitcoms) and Soap Operas

Now these are bywords of television addiction. It seems every time TV producers run out of creative juices, they fall back on the sitcom and drag out yet another 30 minutes of life's situations that can be hilariously funny, boring or baffling. Yet, each can be an invaluable insight into British lifestyles: days of yore, uppercrust, pastoral or cockney working class. British humour, whether in sitcoms, soaps or feature films, tend to rely on the verbal assault rather than the slapstick highjinks popular in some American programmes.

The soap operas (some have gone on for years, like *Coronation Street*) reflecting contemporary lifestyles, replete with unintelligible accents (to the foreigner at least), can be viewed in an educational light. Even if at first you do not understand what is going on. Heavy on the argot, colloquialism, British domestic crises or rural pastiches, some are eminently watchable once you overcome the culture shock barrier. It is life, warts and all, as British producers are chary of too much artificiality. For one thing, glossies like *Dynasty* are more expensive to produce and, if they bomb, a lot of money goes down at the same time as the ratings. The few soaps that pop up occasionally are generally tempered with salt-of-the-earth characters as if to inject reality into fantasy. These are no way near the American snaps that would have us believe every woman goes to bed with full make-up on!

The classics, yes. A British actor would give his eye teeth to appear on stage in a Shakespeare play for a pittance rather than earn a fortune making a cameo in *Dallas*. At least those who respect their craft and can afford not to bite the Hollywood gilded carrot. As one British actress was heard to say, "Why, you never see people in *Dallas* or *Dynasty* ever going to the bathroom!" Real funny is how one can sum up British comedy.

No consensus of opinions, much less an individual, can be arbiter of what constitutes education on TV, in as much as viewers are captive and range from the age of awareness to that when myopia hasn't quite robbed a person of sight. But we are not talking about education *per se*, rather the knowledge which can be gleaned from every programme by a foreigner trying to understand what makes the British tick. Given that the British can be unfathomably quirky, even to other British, the job of television programming is downright difficult.

Quality and entertainment value are therefore secondary, if you regard television as audio-visual reference. Soap operas that reflect contemporary lifestyles, historical documentaries turning back the pages of time, comedies that reflect particular British humour, pro-grammes on art, music and dance, and cops and robbers replete with gore and gratuitous violence are educational, if viewed in this light.

It's as much how you view as what you view that can provide important data to help ease you into the mainstream that will not give cause for bewilderment. British producers of straight contem-porary drama have a penchant for realism, down to the earthy facets of suburban routine, even in a slick, glossy production. In this way, British television differs vastly from its American cousin that rarely ever shows people in other than unreal glamorous settings. British critics are apt to scoff at American imports of which there are relatively few.

A British bobby, after duty, will go home for his tea. An Ameri-can cop slides into his Porsche and drives off to his hilltop mansion. How does he afford it on a policeman's pay? Should television sell escapism or should it be straight from the hip? Whatever your view, it must be appreciated that too much gloss can stick as too much re-alism provides little relief from life's tedium. Fortunately, British TV sits somewhere in between these extremes.

What is refreshing is the fact that British TV and its stars are easy to relate to, making one feel that fame and fortune are that much more attainable. This proclivity for showing life, warts and all, can only give hope to millions that, one day, they can be up there too. Perhaps it is the very tenet of television realism that rubs off on its actors, altogether not a bad thing.

Feature Films

The lack of good, current feature films is a bone of contention among many British viewers. While I tend to agree with this, the question of subjectivity again rises to the fore. The BBC tends to drag out old films which it may well believe to be classics and therefore good for the people. Someone paying £60 a year licence fees may want a steady diet of *Indiana Jones* blockbusters. Then again, those old chestnuts from the *Carry On* stable are still popular with the general public and get prime time over such overpriced and overdone epics like *Star Trek I, II, III, IV*.

On average, over four channels, you get a choice of at least three feature films every evening. And if you should be so inclined, sit up and watch Carlton TV that usually has several feature films between 1 a.m. and 5 a.m.

Come Christmas, the four channels pull out all the stops and hit you with an avalanche of movies, some traditional regulars like *A Christmas Carol* and others of epic adventure. From 23 December to 2 January, every home with a TV set is like the local cinema gone mad. I find it difficult to decide whether to go out or stay in because there are no less than half a dozen films and as many extravaganzas and musical specials to sit through every single day throughout the season. TV wins out invariably over going out. Everything is shut tight for three days over Christmas and wakes up sleepily only after the New Year. Your TV set becomes a real friend. It is also when video shops clean up. Be armed with at least two dozen blank tapes just to tape the Christmas offerings for your own repeats.

Travel Shows

Annual holidays being big business, television naturally sets itself up as a consumer watchdog and you get regular series telling you about the where, when, what and how. In fact, travel programmes spare no expense in production with entire crew and presenters hopping from hot spot to hot spot, giving viewers the real lowdown on value for money. Most are entertaining and informative while a few seem like so much indulgence on the producer's part. It's all very well to titillate the travel taste buds with exotic delights of a Caribbean paradise and quite another to overcome the problems and budgetary juggling to get there. Thankfully, there are few such esoteric travelogues within the consumer slot, being better relegated to the documentary genre.

Live Shows

Usually inane quiz shows that tax no more than one's ability to add up the cost of products in a supermarket trolley. One series, *The Price is Right*, was a weekly free-for-all where the audience had to guess the cost of items. If they got them right, they won the products. It didn't matter that critics panned it as mindless; week after week, it had millions riveted to their sets.

Then there are the traditional Royal Command performances live from Her Majesty's Theatre, variety shows, panel games, talk shows and symposiums that can range from sobre discussions on nuclear physics to chaotic political fracas. There is an endless queue for tickets to these live shows, but you can write in to the BBC or Carlton TV and expect to wait for months.

Two variety shows that annually cause critics to unsheath their claws are the *Eurovision Song Contest* and the countrywide talent-time quest, *New Faces*. For some inexplicable reason, though millions love them, entertainment writers seem to derive sadistic pleasure in tearing them apart.

News

British news dissemination is first class. Little that happens of national import gets past the news hounds. Tragedies, high drama, crime and some frivolous pursuits – in short, news that the public wants – get air time and up-to-the-minute presentation from 6 a.m. onwards. British TV newscasters are virtual stars in their own right and earn wacking salaries for their skills. £300,000 a year is not unknown among the crack journalists, for journalists they really are.

Not simply readers. What you see is 20 minutes of condensed news produced by a large team, writing and pruning the vast amount of information that inundate the TV studios every hour of every day.

More and more world news is being shown, dispelling the belief that British television is insular and provincial. However, local news still constitutes the main bulk of news bulletins for the British are more interested in knowing about what is happening in their own country.

The main bulletins are at 9 a.m., 1 p.m., 6 p.m. and 9 p.m. on BBC 1, and 7 p.m. and 10 p.m. on Carlton TV. BBC 2 and Channel 4 give less priority to news.

Presentation is slick, short, sharp and concisely relevant and with a naturalness reminiscent of American style presentation. British TV newsreaders take most things in their stride, faux pas and all, without going into a panic. Once, the BBC news studio was invaded by a lesbian protestor who somehow chained herself to the newsreader's seat! The reader, Sue Lawley, simply glanced at the invader and carried on calmly with an off the cuff remark that "we seem to be invaded."

Open University

Not just for latter day eggheads, this TV production is very watchable in its objective. Mature students, anybody from taxi drivers to housewives, can put their academic mettle to the test after boning up on a chosen subject. Again, it triggers off responses in the viewer that make him want to dive into the nearest library and catch up on lost opportunity and book learning. Inspirational is the word here, obscure though some of the subjects may be. What the programme does is give hope to people to better themselves. Whether you actually end up on the small screen is the by the by, though to win the Open University award must be akin to earning honours at an institution of high learning.

Sports

Every weekend and all weekend, TV covers every possible sport that is enjoyed by the masses or a few. Most Saturday and part of Sunday afternoons are devoted to sport of one kind or another.

Religious Programmes

Sunday evenings give ample coverage to religious – predominantly Christian – programmes, songs of praise and evening worship type mainly.

Ethnic Programmes

A few hours each week are given to Indian films or art programmes covering the culture. Occasionally you get an old Hong Kong costume drama invariably badly dubbed in American English!

Radio

Far from being overshadowed by television, British radio is alive, well and very listenable. With more than 20 stations to tune in to, you're spoilt for choice. From the talk show-only BBC radio 4 to outrageous independent – even pirate – stations, programmes and broadcasting styles run the gamut from high-brow to plain rudeness.

As an information service, radio is vital to millions of commuters dependent on up-to-the-minute travel and weather reports. In a country where sudden turns of the weather and nasty traffic snarl-ups can make mincemeat of journey plans, British radio is an essential lifeline. For entertainment, it offers tremendous value even over television, with so many stations to tune in to. In the wilds of nowhere, a transistor set triumphs over the idiot box.

Virtually every television personality received his early training in radio and many prefer to stay in radio despite the visual glamour of the small screen. Radio disc jockeys attain as much cult status as their TV cousins do, often getting paid as much. The top voices can earn up to £100,000 a year. One former radio star, Terry Wogan, who now fronts his own chat show three times a week on TV, is reputed to earn in excess of £500,000 a year!

ENTERTAINMENT
Stage

London is the sparkling gem in the diadem of Britain's theatrical heritage; but small towns throughout the country are not exactly entertainment wastelands either. Local playhouses abound and amateur productions by hobbycraft thespians provide good entertainment. Come Christmas, the heritage of Pantomime hilarity is given full mirth with any number of professional productions, some featuring international names usually in the role of the peripatetic 'Dames'. Many actors would give anything to get into a hooped dress, furbelows and warpaint just to get the family screaming with laughter. It is probably the best known of British entertainment genres, a national tradition in fact.

Amateur or professional, they give 100% entertainment value even if the props leave much to be desired. The desire to 'tread the

boards' must be a great buzz for Dustin Hoffman recently gave up a few weeks of his expensive time to star in *The Merchant of Venice* on the London stage.

As a theatrical cornucopia, London's West End is outstanding for both choice and the vicissitudes of getting tickets! It draws audiences from all over the world by the planeload, especially from America. It was crisis time some years ago when American tourists decided to give England a miss after many Middle East political upheavals threatened their travel safety. Theatre companies reeled in shock at the drastic drop in business. Locals rejoiced at the ease of getting tickets.

Under normal circumstances, one has to book months ahead for a hit show, even given that there are no less than three dozen different shows going on at the same time each night.

The most practical solution is to plan your theatre night as far ahead as possible, to avoid disappointment. There are ticket agents dotted all over London, in department stores and within the ranks of shifty touts lurking outside every theatre. But be warned that you might pay up to several times the actual value.

Prices can vary greatly depending on your astute forward planning, ignorance or sheer desperation. Expect to pay at least £18 for a second line show and £40 for a hit.

Generally, agents charge a small booking fee. Booking direct on the phone with your credit card also entails a fee which is between £1 and £4. Queuing up at the box office avoids this, but the chances are you won't get the seats you want because, as luck would have it, the person in front of you just bought the last ticket.

If you're going alone, a good bet is to wait outside the theatre half an hour before showtime and pounce on cancellations. There is a half price booth for theatre tickets at Leicester Square, but the trouble is they're mostly for the least popular shows and there is still the problem of endless queues.

One cardinal rule about theatre going, whether in London or the provinces, is, don't be late. Firstly, it's annoying to others already seated and secondly, you might be stopped from going in until the next interval! I was late once for *Cats* and had to sit outside in the lobby watching the opening minutes on a TV monitor. Most shows start at 8 p.m., so allow yourselves plenty of time to travel, especially if you're going a fair distance.

Cameras and other photographic equipment are not allowed in all theatres. Neither is smoking. Interval time is usually 15 minutes, enough for a quick puff if you must, perhaps a drink at the bar or some ice cream.

In the region outside the West End where almost all theatres are within walking distance of each other, there are also theatres. Wimbledon, Hampstead and Hammersmith boast of theatres of no mean repute. For one thing, many West End bound productions try their act out in these out-of-the-way places first. But far from being 'rehearsal venues' they are bona fide theatres, often putting on first-rate productions that don't get the same media hype.

Because of the sheer volume of visitors, West End theatres have a captive audience all year round. Some productions bomb out after a short run, but by and large they run and run.

The Theatre Heritage

Britain's theatre heritage goes back hundreds of years – to the time of Shakespeare when theatres in the round were common public entertainment. Actors played on an open stage with audiences sitting or standing all around. One such theatre, the Globe, was recently excavated in London and believed to date back to the 15th century. Many leading lights of the theatre are lobbying for the remains of the Globe to be preserved and built up again in the face of threatened development.

Most actors would not consider themselves successful until they have appeared on some West End stage. It's regarded as the sternest testing ground for talent, though the money they earn is a fraction of

203

what television and films offer. Nonetheless, many would gladly give up mega salaries just for a small role in a top West End hit.

And if you're good enough to be accepted by the Royal Shakespeare Company, the world is literally your stage. The best names in show business have at one time or another appeared with the RSC.

Britain produces more actors than its theatres can offer roles to. At any given time, some 90% of them are unemployed or between roles. What do jobbing actors do while waiting for that great role? They work at anything they can get – waiters, salesmen, buskers – and the waiting for most of them can take years.

Such is the lure of the theatre that many will gladly starve and work at jobs that do not bind them down just in case the phone rings and a role is up for grabs. Dancers do the same grinding rounds of auditions in the hope that the next one will be it. Most come with impeccable credentials: graduates of such well-known drama schools

There is no dearth of entertainment in Britain, particularly in London's West End where all the big stars dream to perform.

as the Royal Academy of Dramatic Arts, Italia Conti School, Central School of Speech and Drama and others too numerous to mention. Professional standards are among the highest in the world, but the profession is one of the most precarious.

Television productions, especially soap operas, have been the saviour for many talented people who might get a series or two, or a walk-on part. Exposure is the name of the game and nothing is more than forgettable than not being in the public eye. Stories of 'discoveries' are legend where some young talent is plucked from obscurity and thrust into the global sphere through a major film. It is the stuff of thespian dreams. But theatrical life is far from stardust. Those in the profession moan about the constant grind of doing six shows a week plus one or two matinées. Their lives revolve around their work, with little time for leisure during a production's run, which may be anything from two weeks to years.

For anyone visiting or living in Britain, soaking up the theatre is a priority that must not be missed. It is sheer joy to see a first-class production, great music, acting and glitzy entertainment that is worth all of £20 for two hours. Unlike one-dimensional cinema, live theatre gives one an incredible buzz with its rapport and technical brilliance in many productions.

A current doyen of theatre, both in Britain and America, Andrew Lloyd Webber produces incredible shows that have become a byword. Anyone who has seen *Cats*, *Evita*, *Starlight Express*, *Phantom of the Opera*, *Aspects of Love* and any one of the dozens he has presented will know the genius of this man. *Starlight Express* cost him £1 million just for the stage. And what a stage! Ramps, cantilevered runways, bridges that rise and fall, back projection screens circle the audience, and every member of the cast is on roller skates simulating train engines. Action is all around in a combination of projections, live action, pyrotechnics and stunning routines.

As a cultural offering, British theatre offers a unique insight into the life and mores of the British people. Restoration, contemporary

205

straight plays, comedies, musicals, operettas and avant garde theatre echo much about historical, social and political Britain in the most entertaining way. It beats reading musty tomes in a library!

One of the best ways to understand the quirky British sense of humour is to see a comedy. The first-rate ones give rare insights into what tickles the British funny bone with a wealth of slick one-liners, wry humour and brilliant wit.

Musicals are a showcase of talent with some of the best dancing you can see anywhere in the world. Classical productions breathe life into great literary works by such luminaries as Chekov, Shakespeare, Coward and Feydeau.

There is no lack of realism in British theatre – not least the ones that dare to stage what others fear will fall foul of the censor. One of the most provocative productions I saw in the 70s was the musical *Hair*. Total nudity was its springboard but done with such finesse and superb choreography that few could take offence.

Technical production can leave you breathless with its sheer wizardry. In the recent musical *Miss Saigon*, the stage contained at different times an Eastern street scene, a military HQ, a disco-theque, a shanty town and a helicopter at full tilt!

Soaking up British theatre rubs off in many ways on one. One cannot fail to be moved by the level of professionalism, talent and production techniques that trigger off positive responses, especially for drama, music and stage production students. The cultural richness aside, British theatre is like an enormous open university where you learn the true meaning of discipline, dedication, artistic passion and the finest points of language.

Concerts

In public areas like London's Covent Garden, tube stations and out-side theatres, buskers provide amusement, often of polished calibre. Indeed, many are would-be professionals hoping for that big break or are between gigs and hone their talents for whatever they can get.

Flautists, violinists, even harpists make the Underground their stage everyday. If they're not drowned out by a saxophonist and his ghetto-blaster accompaniment. Baroque, hip hop, steel band or a capella – they're all for free, or a donation.

There is the lovely British tradition of summer seasons – usually musical variety shows with top billing – at Britain's resorts. Many make it an annual pilgrimage to entertain at places like Blackpool, Brighton, Edinburgh and wherever the British spend their summer holidays. These are generally cheap but excellent value, if a little provincial with their jokes. They don't cater to an international clientele as such and, like the annual Christmas pantomime, are British to the core.

Serious music fans can have their fill of concerts throughout Britain, but especially at London's Barbican where top names are regularly featured all year round. Unlike West End stage shows which are usually booked solid months ahead, those for orchestral and solo performances are generally easy to get and cost about £8 for a good seat.

Top bands at venues like Wembley play to packed houses and tickets have to be booked well in advance if you want to catch the likes of Michael Jackson, Prince and other superstars.

There is the annual Edinburgh Festival with a programme to cater for every taste and Glasgow is rapidly becoming known as Britain's cultural city with regular offerings of quality performances from Shakespeare to Cliff Richard.

Anyone living or even visiting Britain would be doing himself an injustice by not taking advantage of such a plethora of entertainment. This is a country where there is little justification to say one is bored for want of cash to seek entertainment, because money is often not the price – just a little effort. A scan through the daily papers will tell you there is something going on somewhere, for free or within most people's budgets. The entertainment media is an extremely well-oiled machine with any number of specialist publications hitting the stands daily and weekly. Friday papers are usually rife with information on who's doing what, where.

Even the ethnic communities have organised their own video clubs, cinemas and other live shows to cater to Bangladeshi, Chinese or Afro-Caribbean tastes. One is spoilt for choice really and apart from public holidays, there's usually something to entertain everyone from six to 90 every day of the year. Museums, zoos and art galleries hold regular specials, especially during school holiday periods when children are catered for.

SEX AND SLEAZE

No matter what the moral watchdogs do, Britain's sense of liberalism spills over onto the stage so often that it becomes difficult to judge what is justifiable and what is smut.

Nudity, full frontal or partial, is always the issue here but the creative people usually have plenty of reasons to defend their stance. It can be difficult to decide what is bad influence and what is art even with the most liberal. Smashing up a guitar on stage may be hailed by the teenyboppers as right, but it can cause apoplexy in adults to think such violence is condoned.

Four letter words are allowed in some films and not in others. At some times and not others. The rules are a veritable quagmire and it boils down to personal dictates. Children under the stated age are not allowed to see films not rated for general entertainment but many cinema operators simply close one eye. Other cinemas cater exclusively to a taste for soft porn (especially in London) boldly endorsing the freedom of choice. Classification is like this:

- U – for universal viewing with no restrictions to age. Films in this category are not likely to offend sensibilities or ethnic cultures.
- PG – with parental guidance for those under 15 years of age. In practice, some cinemas simply ask the age of a young person who is accompanied and do not insist on proof if the parent states he or she is over 15. Films under this category may contain swear

words, some gratuitous violence and subtle sex, but nothing explicit.

- 15 – this category bars anyone under 15 with or without parents as the film has explicit sex, violence and other elements deemed unsuitable and likely to adversely influence young persons.
- 18 – those under 18 are not allowed to view these films as they contain explicit sex scenes, gore and violence. You are likely to be asked for proof of age at cinemas showing films of this rating.

Television is probably the most watched in terms of moral values but what passes as acceptable for the British may not for another race. Neither should one judge British moral values by one's own standards. People from different cultures with different attitudes are not likely to see eye to eye about this issue. Keeping an open mind is the best stance to take. Don't get huffy if you see semi-nudity on TV – it's totally acceptable here, if in context, and does not mean decadence, at least not to the British. Nor should they regard you as prude for objecting to what you feel is beyond good taste. If nudity *per se* upsets you, don't watch. But don't be overly critical.

TRANSPORT
Road

History buffs wil be delighted to know that some of the best roads in Britain were laid during the Roman times. After Julius Caesar had cast his beady eye on the island in 55 BC, the Roman empire began to spread in ancient Britain. Past masters at town building, the Romans also laid down a magnificent network of roads the better to transport their armies with.

Over the centuries these same roads were expanded, laid over and generally stretched to cover much of Britain. There is now a network of motorways, secondary roads and country lanes that makes the country a motorist's dream.

Unless you work in the centre of London, driving is a pleasure in Britain. Cars are not too expensive to come by, and the road network is very comprehensive.

Sign-posting, if not always succinct to the visitor, is nonetheless clear and easy to follow. By far the most speedy means of getting anywhere in Britain by car are the motorways, marked with the prefix letter M. The M1 is a major motorway, the A1 a secondary road – in fact, a dual carriageway for almost its entire length, turning into a motorway, called ingeniously A1(M) in stretches – and the B323 a winding rural road. Arm yourself with a good map of Britain, map out your route beforehand and there are virtually no places in the country you cannot get to.

Do observe motorway driving rules. Take the left lane if you are going at a leisurely pace, the middle lane at an average speed of 60 mph (96 kilometres per hour) and the right lane for overtaking. Speed limits vary from area to area but motorway limits are 70 mph (112 kilometres per hour), though most drivers seem to be clipping ahead at something like 100 mph (160 kilometres per hour). As of going to print, Britain has not gone metric on the road.

It's not just flouting the law and being fined heavily, but the dangers in speeding are ever present. In winter and during bad weather, skidding at even 40 mph (64 kilometres per hour) can cause horrendous pile-ups and even death. At twice this speed and involving juggernauts, the consequences can be devastating. Such is the human failing that a clear stretch of straight road means an all out burst of speed. Beware the oil patch ahead before it's too late.

Despite the network, holiday time can be horrible on the motorways for even these multi-lane ribbons can be choked with traffic that often creeps to a virtual standstill. Add to this the other elements of inclement weather, irresponsible driving, bottleneck tunnels and half the country going on holiday at the same time, and you get a nightmare picture of urban strangulation by automobile.

Services are generally well-strung out along most motorways and there will be signs telling how far it is to the next service station. There are as yet no services on the M11. If for any reason you have to pull up on the side, make sure it's on the 'hard shoulder', a patch designated for such a purpose on the very left hand side. You can only stop for reasons of mechanical breakdown – just having a rest or a quick 'hedge-hop' could land you a hefty fine. Otherwise it can be dangerous with cars whizzing inches past you.

Once off the motorway, roads leading into the towns narrow down; here beware of the one-way systems for which British towns are notorious. You often go round in circles trying to find some place that you can actually see ahead of you. Stop and ask for directions as most locals will untangle you. There is no short cut to learning Britain's road system – it takes regular driving and knowing the shocks to come that you learn to navigate.

Emergency phones can be found along all motorways and they can be operated only by an AA membership key or if you ring the police for help. Never drive for long distances without making sure your car is in good nick, you have a spare tyre, proper tools and an extra blanket or two in cold weather in case of breakdown. It may sound like an evacuation exercise, but better be safe than sorry.

Car Ownership

Unlike living in sprawling suburbs of big countries like Australia or America where public transport does not provide a comprehensive network, living in Britain does not really necessitate owning a car. It is a great pleasure, though, to be able to drive out into the country every weekend at a moment's notice. Car prices are generally   affordable.

A decent 1600 cc car, brand new, will set you back about £9000 and about half this for a second hand one. Because of strict regulations, most second-hand cars are in good condition and save you a walloping amount in capital loss when you decide to sell.

You could even get a 1000 cc, four or five-year-old car for as

Parking laws are very strict in Britain. Even a non-motorised vehicle can be clamped for parking illegally.

little as £500, but the cost of overhauling it could be prohibitive. Many tourists buy such a jalopy, drive all over Europe for several months and abandon it in the knowledge that they've had their money's worth!

Of course most people buy on instalment and pay over one, two or three years. It's not the cost of a car, but maintenance that gets expensive. Normal service after your first free one, if it's a new car, costs an average of £90. Comprehensive insurance works out between £250 per year to anything up to £12,000 depending on your age. The younger a driver is, the higher the insurance. Road tax is another £150 or so. Petrol is getting more expensive by the minute and hovers around £2.00 per litre. A full tank for about £20 can get you from London to Cambridge and back with some to spare. Compare this with train tickets for 5 people at £15 return and you realise the economy of a car.

Every time you renew your road tax, your car has to pass the roadworthy MOT (Ministry of Transport) test. It could be six months or a year, depending on when you renew and for how long. This costs between £15 and £25 depending on where you go. And most garages do MOT as you can see from the sign displayed. It takes but a few minutes if there are no major problems like faulty brakes. New cars do not need to take the MOT for their first three years.

If your car is roadworthy, the other essential is your spare tyre. It could be miles between stations and having a flat in the middle of nowhere, at night, without a spare is a nightmare. The cardinal rule in Britain is to check all systems and tools before setting out on a long trip. Motorway signs tell you what services are available and how far away; so keep a sharp lookout.

In inclement weather, your heater and windscreen wipers must be in mint condition or it could spell trouble. As a check list, the following should always be in your boot all year round:
• Warm blanket
• Battery water
• Anti-freeze

- De-icing spray or scraper
- Jump-start lead (hope to hail a passing car)
- Basic first-aid box
- Torchlight
- Your AA membership card and telephone key. AA emergency phones are dotted along most motorways. The RAC (Royal Automobile Club) is another motoring service club with much the same facilities.
- A good road map of the country
- Small change for public phones
- Driving licence (always carry this with you)

In case of accidents:

Depending on the severity, always pull up on the hard shoulder, and either telephone for help if you can or flag down passing motorists. DON'T simply stop in mid-traffic to argue it out with the car you are involved with. Simply take each other's details and make a report.

Car Washing in Britain

Don't think that washing your car is a cinch. During all but the warmest months, your fingers could get frostbite from the cold water. Far better to spend £1.50 in a car wash once every few weeks or when your car gets dirty. It is quite important to keep your car clean during snowy weather, when local boroughs put grit on the roads to prevent skidding and to melt snow. This can, with time, start to corrode car bodywork. You don't have the problem of excessive heat here but getting into a car in winter can be just as painful. If you happen to have a garage, it makes all the difference in the wintry mornings without the half-hour ritual of warming up both engine and interior. Most petrol kiosks and motoring shops sell woolly seat covers for extra warmth and it's worth getting a set if your original is basic upholstery.

Anti-Theft

Last but not least, invest in an anti-theft alarm. Like in any urbanised country, car thieves are always looking out for careless owners.

Coaches

One of the cheapest and most common forms of travel in Britain if one of the slowest. There are hundreds of coach companies that do day and overnight trips for minimal cost. Many have full facilities like toilets, video and even hostess service for long hauls. Check with the local British Tourist Association (BTA) office for addresses or look through the *Yellow Pages*. Coaches often get you to places that trains don't and are ideal for long trips if you don't drive.

Buses

Perhaps more than any other symbol of Britishness, the red doubledecker bus has come to represent the nation in the most unlikely forms. Together with the phone box, bobby's helmet, the Union Jack and pillar-box, this trundling vehicle has been metamorphosed and shrunk into china saving boxes, chocolate cartons, table mats and dozens of other Britannia collectibles.

The cheapest form of travel, if not the fastest, the British bus has been subjected to many changes in the past decade. First there were cheery conductors – clippies – who knew passengers by their first names and went out of the way to help the old and feeble. Many have been phased out and replaced by one-man-operated vehicles where the driver collects the fares at the door.

Not all the public are happy with this system and there are several reasons. There is an inevitable delay at every stop and the driver is usually brusque and indifferent to the needs of old people who have trouble getting on and off.

Routes are constantly changing because of much motorway and flyover construction which confuses the majority of elderly passengers. Weekend services are frequently disrupted or stopped alto-

Buses are cheap and easy to take, although they are not very punctual. London's red double-decker is one of the symbols of Britain.

gether with industrial disputes over pay and working hours. Many old people who only leave their homes on Sundays to go to church find this a great disappointment. Certain cities have already begun to privatise bus services.

Where it counts, the British bus system provides an essential service in areas where there are no trains, few taxis and (in Greater London) where the tube does not reach. Fares start at around 30p which is roughly half that of the tube and in provincial districts, it is even cheaper.

When you see a Request Stop sign, it means exactly this. Put your hand out, otherwise the bus might pass you by. Most services run at 15 minute intervals though the timetable is often not adhered to. Night buses are a boon in cities where tubes and trains stop running after midnight. A check with the local transport office will tell you what these are.

WEATHER

A topic and an unpredictability that never cease to enthral. It is a subject held forth with equal fervour in the most sumptuous of salons and by down-and-outs on their patch of pavement. The British talk about it so much because there is so much to talk about. 'Will it rain?' brings on great discourse about the comparative relia-bility of raincoats and umbrellas. It is a major query that has direct bearing on the well-being of every individual. Impending rain means a dive into the deeper recesses of your wardrobe for suitable rain-wear, boots and whatever else is necessary to battle this wet ele-ment. Not being prepared means you're exposed to sudden change in weather that can be irksome when you're somewhere miles from the nearest shelter.

And because warm, dry sunny days are often a rare premium in these isles, the sun's benign smile on the land brings out the best in people. Caught without a trusted 'brolly' when the British rain comes down in continuous, cold, chilly drizzle, even the most sanguine temperament is taxed. People's mood swings are to an extent dependent on the weather, so you are less likely to find a stranger in forthcoming mood if it's damp and dreadful.

Be advised never to leave the house without first checking the weather forecast, especially during the colder months of the year which are generally between October and March. You may end up with pneumonia if you are caught unawares.

British weather can be infuriatingly unpredictable, uncomfortable, endlessly grey, glorious and magnificent depending on nature's whims and your own disposition. Yes, there can be pristine beauty in a cold, grey day if you have the soul of an artist, a robust constitution and a positive attitude.

Official dates aside, as they don't mean anything, the four seasons are roughly divided thus:
• Spring: late March to May
• Summer: June to August/September
• Autumn: September to November
• Winter: December to February.

And early spring, despite a beauty that has inspired the greatest poets to extol the splendiferous sight of banks of daffodils nodding their buttery-yellow heads in the sparkling air, can be nippy. Be advised to have a sweater with you – in case a pre-autumn gust cuts through your ribs. It's a time when Britain's splendid flora comes to life, when people take on a joie de vivre which is quite heartening to watch. When the darling buds of May waft their glorious scents and the sky is an incandescent blue, the spirits soar.

Daffodils, crocus and tulips herald this season of flowers, but please do not pick any that grow in public places. The temperature hovers anywhere between 12° and 18° C (54° to 64° F).

Summer is hazy, lazy Sunday afternoons; half naked people in the park soaking up what are invariably fleeting rays of the beloved sun. I have never seen people worship the sun so much, to the exclusion of even work. In the heat of a baking summer day, office workers would drag their lunchtime, doff their outer clothes and spread themselves on the grass in a park, on a verge, anywhere that catches the rays of warmth and blithely ignore the passing of time.

It is a time for glorious fruit harvests, for many farms open to the public to pick their own fruit for a pittance. There is nothing quite like picking sun-ripened apples, pears and plums then. Farm owners find it more remunerative to let you pick your own rather than pay workers to do so.

It can get hot, like in 1989, reputed to be the hottest in 60 years. It went up to around 30° C (the high 80s F) and in some places, beyond 30° C (90s F). Thank goodness it is not humid, and come evening, it always cools down. The only stifling places to be in in summer are packed train carriages and the kitchen. The curious, and welcoming, thing is it's cooler indoors and in basement areas where there is ample ventilation.

Summer also means endless crowds because all the schools break for the longest holidays of the year – up to 12 weeks – and every resort, spa, tourist attraction is bursting at the seams. Book your holidays well in advance – six months preferably – to enjoy your break without the hassle of uncertain accommodation.

If you're staying put, this is the time to do battle with the creepy crawlies. Britain is not known to have them in abundance but come a warmer than normal summer, flies, gnats and ants pop up. For most of the year they seem to disappear somewhere.

Generally dress lightly, shorts being practical gear when out driving on weekends. This, however, is not a favourite form of wear among the British who would choose lightweight trousers – only trendy young people will sport them. Remember that it can cool down considerably in the evening.

From April onwards, the days are long and it stays bright until 10 p.m. in July. Temperatures average 18° to 26° C (64° to 79° F). Summer weather is never predictable, and some years are full of rain, others can be cold. Never travel far without a sweater and

As the leaves drop from the branches, the ground takes on all shades of yellow, red and brown. Autumnal scenery is serene and golden.

either a waterproof raincoat or an umbrella – better safe than sorry. In northern Scotland in summer, even when the sun shines, you can feel a chill in the wind, and a thick sweater is essential.

Autumn is a specially beautiful time if you live in the country. The colours of trees range from tawny gold to russet and glowing auburn, and the late evening sun casts a stunning glow on every blade and leaf.

The air is clear, sparkling though chilly, and does not quite have the bite of winter. The shops will have brought out their corduroys and wools by early September and be advised to have a coat with you at all times. Most flowers begin to die then but the rainbow colours are replaced by the autumn hues that inspired such great artists as Constable and Gainsborough to put their magic on canvas. Temperatures begin to dip to as low as 12° C (54° F).

If you are lucky enough to have a really good summer, central heating would have been turned off by May and need not come on again till mid-September.

Winter really begins to bite in January, though December can be cold – if not cold enough to have a White Christmas. Much as it is a lovely idyll, this is rare and in eight years I have had the pleasure of falling snow at Christmas only once. And then it was briefly, not enough to build snowmen and have snowball fights. The flakes start to come down in January and February, and the sight of one's first snowfall is pure wonder.

Like clouds of cottonwool, the snowflakes make you want to run out and catch them in your hands and look up at this scene of winter wonderland. Until your third winter. When the magic palls a little and you begin to swear at the slush of the first melt, when everything turns to mush. And somehow, even the prettiest swirling snow shower loses its charm!

French windows condense with the dripping chill and it can be quite a job mopping up. Extreme cold plays havoc with the machinations of a household – pipes freeze, metal window and door frames stick and the smallest crack lets in icy draughts that congeal the hottest stew in minutes.

If you do not have central heating, make sure every room has an electric or gas heater. Your heating bills will more than double and taking a bath or shower is an exercise in aerobatic dexterity. Emerging from a hot shower, you can get chilled if you don't climb fast enough into a bathrobe. Heated bath rails for towels are a comfort.

Sometimes it seems you can't wear enough layers to keep you warm. The best option is to have a really warm coat instead of wearing multiple layers when outdoors. A cotton or wool vest next to the skin is good insulation. Having to wear coat, scarf, hat and gloves can be cumbersome and it's best to acclimatise quickly by braving the elements in small doses. It took me about a year but by my third winter I could do without a scarf on all but the coldest days.

During your first year you are likely to go mad and buy things like ankle warmers, muffs, chunky sweaters and boots. As your body adjusts you'll find most of these quite unnecessary except as a fashion statement. The thing is to buy a sensible wardrobe that sees you through nine months of the year. You can make expensive mistakes like splashing on a costly leather jacket that is really no better than a sensible wool jacket at half the price.

Winter can be a time of great content, drinking hot chocolate by a roaring (gas!) fire and huddling into a thick robe to watch television. Few houses other than those in the country and farms have live fires as solid fuel is hard to come by. Britain's famous fogs in the last century were caused largely by coal fires and laws were passed to outlaw open hearths in all but the most rural of places. The toxic peasouper fogs went by the middle of this century. You still get the occasional fog but nothing like the yellow scourge that spawned so many Sherlock Holmes stories.

Before winter sets in, check all your systems. It can be distinctly uncomfortable when your old boiler breaks down in mid-winter and repairmen cannot get to you immediately – like on weekends. It pays to service all heating and insulating systems regularly.

The past several years have seen the usually predictable British climatic four seasons behave erratically. Green issue people blame it on the rape of the ozone layer but whatever the reason, there have been strange turns. One summer stretched into autumn and winter never really took hold. Another winter was so bad it crippled the country and hurricanes and gales, not usually a part of the temperate climate, lashed down with unfamiliar ferocity. The weathermen's consensus is that British weather has become unpredictable and world weather appears to be warming up. What the future bodes, if indeed the ozone layer is to blame, is a frightening prospect. Comment has been made by scientists that if the world weather gets any warmer – by a few degrees even – London, New York, Sydney and many other cities could be under water.

Weather Reports

More than enough reason for a nation to be overly concerned with the weather. And when they are caught unprepared, the weathermen are the ones who get the blame. For example, when the Met office for some inexplicable reason did not or could not predict a hurricane, they met with a people's wrath equal to that of the howling elements.

There are weather reports on radio and TV frequently everyday, usually following the news that give fairly detailed breakdowns of where's dry, wet, sunny, dull, hot or cold, and normal temperatures. Some weather reports also cover European forecasts for the benefit of travellers. This is relevant if you make frequent trips especially by sea or air.

Bad weather often means flight cancellations, and sailings, though not as badly affected, can be extremely uncomfortable in squally weather. Newspapers have weather reports on a less detailed basis but are a reliable indication of what to expect.

HOLIDAYS

Now here's something of a sacred pursuit on a scale that never fails to send shock waves across the British Isles come summer and bank holiday weekends. These are gazetted national off days and always on Mondays. Travel companies must advertise their delicious offerings (some hidden truths read like horror stories) more fiercely in Britain than anywhere else.

When people take their holidays, weekend jaunts or day-return trips en masse, roads, rail, sea and air routes naturally clog up and it can be a nightmare. The newspapers are full of such stories at peak season.

Another menace are travel company shysters and sloppy organisation. Headlines scream on about families booked on package trips that promise all and deliver precious little. What's more, many families save for months – even years – booking equally far ahead

223

only to find their two weeks an exercise in wretched frustration. If this paints a ghastly picture, it's perfectly true, year after year. With millions of pounds in the offing for travel companies, there will naturally be cowboy outfits without the slightest conscience about fleecing clients. Common is the story where such fly-by-nights set up shop, take their money and run, leaving their victims with no-go packages. It must have been with wry mirth that one company advertised on their hoarding: "You've tried the cowboys, now try the Indians." They were Indian travel agents.

Overbooking is a common cause followed closely by timetables that eat into precious time, not leaving enough for travellers to recoil from their travails. These journeys into the unknown can befall almost anyone constrained with budgets that disallow booking the more upmarket tours. And there are literally hundreds of small companies offering 'two weeks of paradise in Costa del Sol'.

It's imperative you buffer yourself against the following shocks:

- Book your holiday months ahead. The Brits do – not just weeks, sometimes even a year ahead.
- Never take holiday brochures (especially continental packages to the British-swamped countries of Spain and Greece) at face value. Check for cheap loopholes. Cut price usually means cut everything else – from bug-ridden beds to foul food.
- Boats, trains and planes are chock-a-block at the best of times given the great British penchant for holidays, and delays of up to two days are not uncommon.
- Read the daily press for horror stories. They don't mince words about appalling accommodation and other travesties. One Spanish hotel advertising "glorious views of the Mediterannean" actually looked out on a hole in the ground where part of the hotel was still being built.
- Travel insurance is a resounding must. Theft and other misadventures are less likely to send you on a tailspin if you can get compensation.

Driving Holidays in Britain

Marvellous though British roads are, they can be car-strangled during peak travel months and bank holiday weekends. Tailbacks on the motorway are so common I usually avoid them when we drive out on long weekends. Take the smaller country roads that are not only less hassling, but your route also offers picturesque views. Motorways, even when clear, are pretty boring.

Don't leave accommodation to chance at such times. Even the tattiest bed-and-breakfast places are full in summer. Get hold of any number of brochures and leaflets from any British Tourist Author-

While driving around in Britain, you can break your journey at any of the charming country inns which dot the countryside.

ity office (every town of tourist interest has one) and book ahead. Most will honour a phone booking.

Pack your own food if your journey is to take more than several hours. Motorway service stations – places to top up car and stomach – are notoriously iffy on food. So too are many roadside chains, though you may chance upon a good, unpretentious transport cafe where lorry drivers can rely on decent meals at very reasonable prices. Otherwise, expect meat and vegetables with lumpy gravy. Or an endless hamburger of microwave mush.

Car hire is relatively cheap in Britain and costs a fraction of train travel if you are in a group that can squeeze into a saloon. Say five people would pay something like £20 per head (petrol and car hire) to drive from London to the Lake District and all over for a week-end, not counting accommodation.

MOT

It simply means Ministry of Transport but in specific reference to the roadworthiness of your car. Any car more than three years old has to have an MOT test before the certificate of roadworthiness can be granted. It doesn't apply to new cars, but when you get your road tax renewal notice, you have to get an MOT done before you can renew it. If your vehicle is basically sound, it should have no problem passing the test which vehicular mechanics will do at garages. This latter reference does not only apply to where you keep your car – it's the general description of car maintenance shops. And MOT costs vary depending on the state of your vehicle.

SPORTS
Football

The British passion for football transcends mere enthusiasm for the sporting life. Since its invention some 125 years ago (by the British of course) football has become a national preoccupation, a cult movement almost provoking feelings within the public breast that

For the ardent football fan, there are specialised shops which sell everything he needs to show his support for his favourite club.

range from mere ra-ra support to fierce fanaticism. And along the ugly periphery, loathsome loutish behaviour that has unfairly tarnished the game. In the past half a dozen years, a few boorish fans more intent on creating mayhem than cheering spirit have been receiving more headline press coverage than goal-scoring prowess.

The game has remained much the same as it was since its invention. It is a game of skill based on the player's handling of the ball with his feet or head and is steeped in the tradition of sportsmanship. However, if the players display sportsmanship on the field, the same cannot be said for some of their supporters. British football in the past few years has been plagued by the problem of violence off the pitch. And British football fans have acquired a reputation for loutish behaviour overseas, as their misbehaviour has spilled over the rest of Europe during international matches. During the last World Cup series in Italy, the Italian authorities did not take any chances and deployed so many policemen that the matches resembled anti-riot exercises!

Violence at football matches is a sticky problem of national proportions. Crowd control measures, enforced club membership and police cordons will not always ensure the prevention of volatile behaviour that can lead to disaster.

But the Football Association assures that the game itself remains sacred to the British and unsullied by emotional upheavals around it. There will always be the lout bent on creating chaos, be it a football match or rock concert. It simply means any large gathering of people must need adequate policing as much for likely hooliganism as for smooth flow. The riot syndrome is a volatile one, usually mindless, and it manifests itself when human instincts are reduced to herd levels. It is, however, not a frequent occurrence. It is comparatively rare to experience or even notice any trouble at most football games, and you should attend one to experience this element of British culture, even if you do not support a particular team.

The football season is between August and May each year with games played every Saturday at 3 p.m. and on Tuesday or Wednesday at 7.30 p.m. In England and Wales a major change occurred in 1992 when a new FA Premier League was started, comprising 22 clubs. The remaining 70 full-time professional clubs play in the three main leagues. In Scotland there are 38 clubs, in Northern Ireland, 16 semi-professional clubs play in the Irish Football League. During the season, over 2000 English League matches are played and tickets range from £5 to £25 depending on the division.

As for amateur football, there are 42,000 clubs in England alone, so if you hanker to kick a ball around, there is always a pitch near you. Every county in Britain has a regional football association.

Cricket

There seems to be no middle ground for feelings about this sport from the British public. Either they believe it should be buried deep in the ground or will go to great lengths following the teams around. But not without a selection of novels, carafes of wine, fruit, a rug and pillows to snooze on. After all, what does one do during those endless tests at The Oval? Yet at every cricket season there is madness everywhere with *aficionados* taking French leave from work to cheer the home team and traffic grinding to a halt outside Lord's cricket pitch in Northwest London.

Whether you actually like the game or not is not the issue. The media cover the games in great detail, as well as the behaviour (on and off the pitch) of the major players. Popular sentiment for the game is so high that some players have attained star status.

Polo

A king's sport or for those with money to burn. This premier (read expensive!) sport gets coverage more so because Prince Charles likes his weekly chukkas than the game *per se*. And of course the prospect of rubbing shoulders (or rather horse's shanks) with the rich and famous. Definitely not within reach of the hoi-poloi – it'll cost you plenty to maintain horses, groom, gear and the social cachet indulged by polo circles – but the best way to become a celebrity. Princess Di, it seems, hates the game and puts up with it only because her royal husband is so besotted with it. After all, he can hardly play football or rugby, dribbling and scrumming with the likes of the commoners. In polo, he doesn't have to give his kingdom for a horse especially as his family owns a string of them. Of course the press will wait and watch for every royal tumble or blue language. Prince Philip used to turn the air purple with his language when he was playing. Alas, age has caught up with him and the old princely bones can now only indulge in horse and carriage racing. A very genteel sport – except for the poor sweating horses.

Swimming

Unless you're seriously into lapping for Olympic honours, this sport is not the most comfortable for those unaccustomed to temperatures below 15° C (70° F). There are several indoor (heated but not very warm!) swimming pools in every major city and town charging a small fee for the facilities. Avoid the holiday months of April, August and September when most pools are thick with students. Come autumn (November onwards), unless you're a masochist, swimming is a distinctly chilly experience. In very warm summers, the coastal resorts in the south like Brighton, Bournemouth and Eastbourne offer sea-swimming. But even with temperatures around 30° C (the high 80s F), be prepared for the sea to be still chilblain-inducing. For more information, look in your local directory or the *Yellow Pages*.

Cycling

Outside the cities, Britain is a cyclist's paradise. Probably the healthiest, cheapest and most fulfilling form of transport. For a low outlay of £50 for an average (they can cost up to £500 for souped-up models with 12 gears) bicycle, the country is your pedalling oyster. It is the best way to see Britain if you have the time and calf muscles. British Rail allows you to board with your bicycle, but not the London Underground. It is also wise to wear a safety sash fluorescent green or orange in colour when riding at night, especially along rural areas where street lighting is inconsistent or non-existent. Make sure you have a very strong lock for when you park and chain your bicycle to some secure railing or post. In public parks, look out for signs that prohibit cycling, especially on manicured lawns or flowerbeds. On city roads, there are designated cycle paths, so use them for your own safety. It is not an uncommon sight to see men in suits and well-dressed women cycling to work – at least part of the way. During transport strikes – which can happen any time – your bicycle is invaluable, never mind that you're a judge or banker. The British are unfazed by such irksome hiccups and simply 'get on with it'.

Jogging

There are relatively few designated jogging tracks in Britain for the simple reason that there is a whole country (outside the highly congested city areas) available for this sport. Public parks are your best venues where the air is bracing and you do not run the risk of being knocked down by juggernauts and other motorised vehicles. Given that it's cold 10 months a year, wear warm jogging gear and proper shoes. If you like jogging in company, contact your local sports association or council which will put you in touch with the right people. Once a year, in summer, the London Marathon brings out the zany, eccentric, charitable, passionate and plain nutty jogger to participate in the most colourful and humorous race of all. People in gorilla costumes (even in extreme heat), ballet-tutus, nappies – every conceivable and inconceivable getup – join the fun. The serious joggers will have left them miles behind within minutes but these merry marathoners get the best press inevitably. Behind most of the zaniness lies a good cause as thousands of pounds are raised every year for charity.

A note of caution: It is not prudent to jog alone in out of the way places at night. If you have to, keep within well-lit areas and wear fluorescent sashes. All public parks are closed at sundown. Never jog on motorways.

Walking to Work

The British do not regard walking as a mere ambulatory means of getting from one point to another. Most people from hot climates find walking a chore and take a little getting used to when they have to move thus in Britain. But the climate is entirely conducive to walking and a distance of four or five miles (6.4 to eight kilometres) is a whisker's twitch to serious walkers. On average, commuters chalk up a mile or two each day walking from home to train, tube or bus station and back. Not to mention the distances you have to cover changing stations and negotiating escalators and walkways. It is healthy and rarely uncomfortable unless you're physically feeble. Once you get past the notion that a mile is a mile anywhere, walking in Britain is exhilarating and enlightening. You can discover much more about history, tucked away places of interest and gems of historical interest.

Walking for Pleasure

Almost all of Britain's suburban and rural areas are ideal for serious walking. But be armed with maps, basic medical kit and other life-sustaining items, should you like walking in real country like Cumbria, Scotland, Wales and other craggy highlands. Sensible, comfortable and stout shoes are *de rigueur* especially in the cold months – proper hiking boots should be purchased for serious fell walking, and you should always take waterproof clothing when hill walking in areas such as the Peak District, Yorkshire Dales, Snowdonia and Scotland. Check with local authorities where walkers generally go to and what dangers there are in isolated places.

Walking is a national sport for many and highly recommended for those disinclined to other more vigorous sport. Avoid doing this alone for obvious reasons. And always have some nourishment with you: water, thermos and biscuits, should you lose your way. There are relatively few places in Britain where a public phone or farmhouse is not within a few miles' reach.

Wimbledon

Anyone, it seems, is for tennis during Wimbledon month. Is it all sport you ask? Not on your nelly. It's as much about Chris Evert's lace knickers, strawberries and cream and picnic hampers from Harrods. It seems being actually there is less fun than poring through the tabloids each Wimbledon day to find out who's screaming foul language at whom, who's wearing what and the comparative prices of strawberries at supermarkets and the Wimbledon pitch. All in dead seriousness. Tennis? Wouldn't be the same without the fruit.

Henley Royal Regatta

For four days in early July every year, Britain's premier rowers take to the Thames in a regal boat regatta that dates back 170 years. The first Oxford and Cambridge boat race took place at Henley-on-Thames in 1829. Ten years later it was formalised as an annual festival and in 1855 received the royal stamp when Prince Albert became its patron.

It is a boat race like no other in Britain, or any international boating event for that matter. Participants row upstream because the currents disallow stands to be erected at the finish of a race. It is strictly an amateur affair despite the royal suffix, but the anomaly does not prevent thousands of enthusiasts from turning up each year. And for all this, there is no permanent grandstand or even facilities for spectators.

It's one of those terribly British events steeped in tradition with no rules that correspond to any international ones. Yet, there are Henley regattas in Canada, Australia and America. Such is its anglophile appeal among the *aficionados*.

Henley is not jeans and T-shirt. White trousers, striped blazers and rowing caps are *de rigueur*; an amusing sight to see people of all ages and physical types strutting about looking like sixth form boys. Most have never held an oar in their lives! Like Royal Ascot, ambience is all. It matters little what your nautical inclinations are. Turning up in regulation gear, perhaps with a picnic basket of fruit, wine and pies, will ease you into the spirit of a very British tradition.

Royal Ascot

Britain's royal family are nuts about horses – the irreverent refer to them as the 'horsy set' – and one of their favourite events is the Royal Ascot. Which is really another betting event graced by royalty. Of course the Queen and her family own some of the most splendid stables but the monarch does not bet. The others are free to do so, and they do.

The first race meeting at Ascot Heath in Berkshire was in 1711 and Queen Anne was said to have been present. For the next 50 years, the event seemed to have been forgotten and it was in 1760 that the Duke of Cumberland got it going again. Subsequent members of the royal family added to the sense of prestige and, by the time King George IV came to the throne, attending Ascot had all the trappings of a regal procession.

Today, the Queen and her family travel by car from Windsor Castle and then transfer to her magnificent horse-drawn open landau with a full escort of scarlet-coated outriders. They proceed down the Straight Mile at the start of each afternoon's racing. They make for the Royal Box before which stretches the Queen's Lawn that no one can set foot on. Invitation to the Royal Box is by invitation only by the monarch herself. But if you should be so lucky, you might get into the Royal Ascot enclosure where the minor royals, assorted hangers-on and glitterati mingle. Some 3000 people in Britain vie for this privilege every year.

When once an impeccable lineage and a spectacular wardrobe were essential, this stomping ground is now for the likes of assorted pop stars, nouveaux riches and the odd gate crasher or two.

It is a showcase of the regal, eccentric and serious horse breeders. Milliners come out in full-throated cry to outdo each other with their confections, most of which make the front pages of the daily tabloids. One grand dame of Ascot, Mrs Gertrude Shilling, turns out each year in more and more outrageous hats.

PARKS

Entertainment isn't always the obvious variety. Britain's public parks and private gardens are among the most magnificent in the world and are either for free or for a small charge to cover maintenance. There are dozens of parks that provide much pleasure if your taste is to commune with nature. Every county and city has some kind of park, whether just open ground for romping in or beautifully lanscaped gardens for stunning presentation. Feeding ducks in London's Regent's Park is as therapeutic as it is educational as the birds come from many different countries.

WINDOW SHOPPING

Window displays are an art form, especially in big city stores, which should not be missed. At Christmas, the major department stores usually have animated window displays that are veritable stage shows. I've seen full tableaux of Snow White, Cinderella and other Grimm fairy tales that put to shame some live shows. These marvels of electronic engineering and creativity make shopping a joy in Britain during the festive season.

SOAKING UP THE SUN

Most foreigners, especially the Chinese and Indians, are rather diffident about sprawling on public parks when the sun shines. Perhaps they have had enough sun or are too shy to do what many British do. On glorious summer days, you will see dozens of people in swimwear simply soaking up the warmth in their backyards. Initially, I was bemused by so much sun-worshipping but in time, after years of chill, I began to appreciate this rare commodity in Britain. After all, you can only go bare-chested in public a few months a year. And you won't get arrested as long as you don't bask in the altogether.

NIGHT BIRDS

Alas, Britain is not generally a late-night country. Some big cities have clubs that stay open till 2 or 3 a.m. The licensing laws are strict even in London where there are jazz clubs that cater for dawn-watchers. Transport is the major problem unless you drive, for taxis after midnight can be hideously expensive. Most places shut down by 1 a.m.

Chapter Ten

IN PUBLIC

RACISM

Britain must rank as one of the most aware nations of the insidiousness of real or imagined racism, and the British are extremely sensitive to the needs of the ethnic minorities. When the racism cry is whipped up on the premise of such as the use of the golliwog symbol on a popular brand of jam, bureaucrats must crawl up the wall. This happened not too long ago and the logo has since been banished.

In schools, offices and other organisations where coloured people and other ethnic minorities work among the majority of whites, this sensitivity is never far from the surface. Until recent times, relatively few Chinese worked outside the catering industry and were buffeted from the likely event of racial brouhaha. A century ago, when the first Chinese arrived to work in the docks in the East End of London and in Liverpool, as now, their diligence won the respect and admiration of the British.

West Indians and Indians from the sub-continent, who make up the two largest ethnic minorities, are more liable to be the target of bigotry. However this is largely isolated. West Indians, especially because of widespread unemployment, cultural differences and a historical justification for being uptight, having arrived on British shores as indentured labour, suffer more ignominy. The seeds of racism need but little pellets of fuel to spread. So the vicious circle spreads. It seems incredulous that such colourful entertainment as *The Black and White Minstrel Show* – the mainstay of early vaudeville both in America and here – was axed amid cries of racism. On the other side of the coin, bigotry exists among individuals who must not be seen as reflective of a national attitude.

Racism takes strange forms as in one incident related to me by a friend. One of his father's acquaintances refuses to watch any television with blacks in the cast! "I will not have a coloured person in my parlour!" is his incredible stand. An isolated but nonetheless alarming case of blinkered bigotry.

Time and time again, I have reached out first with a genuine interest in British mores and put all superciliousness and chauvinism in the background. Yet, when confronted with such posers as "Do you eat dog?" it is extremely easy to get huffy and drive the wedge in further.

By and large, Britain has a harmonious polyglot society even in the most remote of counties and towns. Witness at least one Chinese takeaway and Indian tandoori restaurant in every other town or village. The Chinese may not socialise freely but have the highest respect from the majority of British people. This very reluctance to assimilate caused enough concern in 1984 for the Home Affairs

The changing face of the British bobby: an Indian policeman.

Committee to publish a report aimed specifically at the Chinese community. Indians have been in Britain much longer and have assimilated much better. The little newsagents and hole-in-the-wall shops they run have become a permanent, and welcome, feature in most urban cities. Especially on weekends when all other shops are shut tight.

While London is not a yardstick by which to judge cultural cohesion, racial harmony in this great maw rubs off well on other communities. A recent threat that members of the dreaded Ku Klux Klan were about to descend on British soil resulted in a national stand against all racial prejudice.

One has to be careful about ethnic sensitivities when working among minorities. A decade ago when anti-Pakistani feelings ran high, an innocent remark could spark off riots. Like referring to the community as 'Pakis'. "We are Pakistanis, not Pakis" is the furious rejoinder when someone inadvertently uses the term.

Britain welcomes anyone who has the legal right to live, work or study here. What prejudice exists does so in the mental pockets of individuals who, for historical or personal reasons, will not condone non-English amongst their midst. But they are a minority breed.

The so-called British sense of superiority is nothing more than a joke today with the biggest putdown of this superciliousness coming from the British themselves. Another situation of self-effacing diffusion. Often, it is a subservient attitude amid the ethnic minorities that breeds this notion. There are any number of reasons for this – the chief being lack of the English language among migrants. There are thousands who, after more than a dozen years in the country, still cannot speak English. I know of two women from mainland China who emigrated here some 20 years ago. Their children, born here, speak fluent English down to the accent picked up from school mates. The poor mothers can hardly string together two sentences. One managed to make her nationalisation proclamation and got her papers. The other failed and has made no attempt to enrol in night school or otherwise bone up on English. She does not attribute this to her indifference to a fundamental requirement, but that the Home Office is biased!

More seriously, her activities are curtailed as she cannot read English, especially signs on the Underground and train platforms.

Individual incidents of racial intolerance must be viewed in singular light. It is not easy to quell the anger provoked by racial bigotry, but so is that of any other human misdeed. Vandalism, muggings, robbery are all blights of urban living – not racism though the accusation is never far from the surface in communities where migrant populations are extensive. One must put these in proper perspective or run the risk of perpetual anger that is detrimental to peaceful existence in a foreign country.

The Black and White Issue

Every year for the past 24 years, London's Notting Hill Carnival, Europe's biggest street festival, a sort of mini Rio, focuses attention on Britain's considerable Caribbean population. Come late August, this area explodes in a pot-pourri of noise, colour and pulsating rhythms.

The carnival used to be a sparkling festival of music, gorgeous costumes and frenzied camaraderie. In the past several years it erupted into violence and even death, and when white police went into action to stem the fray, the old problem of harassment surfaced again. Another instance of using the racism tag to drive the wedge in between black and white.

The Carnival Entertainment Committee took no chances in 1989 with 1000 police to supervise the three-day event. With the number of people expected to attend numbering some 500,000 a day, anything can – and usually does – happen. It did among a handful of those, probably with too much alcohol and too little common sense, and when the police shut down the festival at 7 o'clock, fury erupted.

Still, leading black figures see the area as a vehicle for black enterprise. The organisers contend that carnivals can be big business – both from catering and spinoffs – and enormous potential for community development. They see it as an economic base obviating the need for local government funding eventually. Sponsorship is welcome but it is a shot in the arm of black pride if the carnival becomes self-sufficient. The objective is to channel the money spent – an estimated £24 million – back into the community pot. The London Boroughs Grant Committee donated £52,000 to the Carnival Committee for a start. There are conflicting views of the carnival. On one side the murmurs accuse it as a 'capitalist sellout'. On the other, it is seen as a gathering of the arts, an example of public safety, community enterprise and good management. If only the hot heads can be contained.

The event each year is waited for with feverish excitement by most of Britain's black communities. The past decade has been witness to much controversial strife, mainly triggered off by such events where white policemen are seen as racist ogres when they attempt to do their job. The 1000 constables on duty every year are almost entirely white. Why the force employs few blacks is another sensitive issue that no one is prepared to elaborate on. On the whole, though much progress has been made in race relations, the problems remain acute.

Reasons

According to statistics, one in three Caribbean families in Britain has a single parent. As incomplete nuclear families, misdemeanours occur frequently among the restless young who have little parental guidance. At a gathering of hundreds of thousands where beer flows and the spirit is high, restless youth can boil over easily.

When the family breaks down, troubles snowball and drugs take vicious hold of many black communities. Council housing estates with a preponderance of single families are particularly susceptible.

241

Most addicts are young, black and are not particular who they steal from and mug. The daily 'fix' is their raison d'être and no one is spared. Family, friends, neighbours, white or black.

Black community leaders remain tight-lipped about the problem and any drug raids are seen as harassment by white policemen.

The heated outcry is one of an 'uncaring and belligerent white society'. When the police raided a Brixton estate a few years ago, there was a vehement outcry from the council leader. She condemned the police for overzealousness and the sensitive issues that erupted caused much whiplash.

Many independent black schools have been established with the objective of shoring up the inadequate educational level of Caribbean children. Local government, the media and private employers are opening more doors to talented black children, signalling the emergence of a black middle class.

Unfortunately, unlike in the Caribbean where extended families embrace single parents without reprobation, it is not the same case in Britain. A youngster growing up in a disruptive environment is likely to view society with scepticism and some anger.

In his book *Behind the Front Lines – Journey Into Afro Britain*, Ferdinand Dennis who won the 1988 Martin Luther King Memorial prize, concluded one thing. Black leaders must demand that their communities take greater responsibility for their own development. Only then will the crisis of all black families in Britain be recognised. Only then will cries of white harassment and other imagined putdowns be seen in their true light of racism-fanning.

VIOLENCE

Well-meaning though the British media mean to be, their reporting of crime can sometimes paint an uglier-than-the-truth picture of violence. One bomb does not make London or any other city in Britain an explosive site. Fatalism aside, Britain is no more a statistical horror story of criminal carnage than any other country with the same urban sprawls, population base and attendant problems.

The popular press tend to make an endless hue and cry over every little eruption, and visitors are frightened out of their wits to even travel on the tube at night. It's easy to be frightened when you read of someone being mugged for £3 but the circumstances need to be considered in depth.

Petty thievery exists everywhere where affluence juxtaposes uncomfortably with joblessness. And it's often the carelessness of the public that creates it.

Tourists are usually the easiest targets. With camera, bags, shopping and all the jetsam of buying sprees weighing you down, and being less alert than usual after a day's tramping, you might as well

wear a sign saying "Pick me, I'm all yours." People WILL keep wallets in their back trouser pockets, women WILL sit in crowded trains with their handbags within easy reach of professional pick-pockets and old people WILL travel alone in lonely stations. In the latter case, perhaps they cannot help it. In most others, they should know better.

There are something like three million jobless in Britain in addition to the thousands of others from the EC with no particular set of ethics about where their incomes come from. The finger of suspicion points only too easily to those most likely to turn to crime. The real reason lies in the lure of millions of visitors to these shores, usually with plenty of cash and valuables practically on public display.

The jobless of course cannot defend themselves because they do not have a strong enough collective voice. In any case it's easy to tarnish the entire lot for the misdeed of one. They're a handy pincushion for all of society's accusatory pricks.

On the whole petty crime – and this constitutes the major cases – does not simply occur if circumstances are not conducive.

Reading about bombs in department stores, in parks and through the post, you can get paranoid about even going to a public toilet if you let it worry you. The truth is Britain is not the hotbed of violence it appears to be from all the pulp press stories.

Political causes, personal vendettas and great railway robberies generally do not touch the lives of the masses unless you happen to be in the way. But then you could be run over by a truck while distracted by some lascivious advertisement in your newspaper.

The IRA are ever willing to take the blame for every bomb blast or murder and only recently, another crude bomb went off in front of a bookshop that emphatically stated it DID NOT stock Salman Rushdie's *Satanic Verses*. It seems a picture of political and religious fanaticism gone haywire. But Britain is a country where passionate causes garner tremendous support. But great passion, political, religious or artistic, can be a two-edged sword. There are followers and detractors. Depending on the degree of emotional upheaval, there will be spit and blood. This is what makes the country interesting. Whether you simply observe or get involved, your destiny lies in your own hands. From simply avoiding potential petty thievery to a religious imbroglio. Common sense, fatalism and plain luck all play a part. You also sharpen your alertness and sense of self-preservation.

Often crime and violent behaviour are the result of frustration. You see a gang of youths 'steaming' down a train from carriage to carriage with time on their hands, perhaps penniless and angry at the whole world. Their criminal bent stops short of actual misdemeanour because at the heart of their volatile behaviour is probably a need for attention.

Knowing this helped allay my fears that I might be a victim. When you see a group of black youths looking like they might close in on you, you could be wrong. They could just as well be clean living people having a social chit-chat. I make this point because of the 'stigma' of being black in this country. One black is aggro, two spell trouble and a group you had better avoid: this is the general consensus of the blinkered public. This is an injustice to the community, not to mention insidious racism.

How to Avoid Trouble

Just a few rules to observe when you settle in Britain.

Avoid getting into an argument with any angry looking youth. He may be looking for a punchbag for his anger at the world. Or your affluence serves to aggravate his deprived situation.

If you have to travel by tube or train at night, make sure you sit in a carriage with several other people.

If you have to get off at a lonely station, keep your wits about you and run like hell if accosted. Or give up your few pounds to avoid being hurt. Unless you're in the position to defend yourself against knives and other lethal weapons, it's more than your life's worth to retaliate. For all your civic-mindedness your principles are no match for a switchblade or gun.

Rape is another matter altogether. There are no easy solutions to this terrible crime. The same rule of thumb must apply. Avoid being in a situation where you are alone with a stranger – respectable though he may appear to be. British Rail are already talking about introducing 'women only' carriages as many women have to travel alone at night. Whether this will come about or will be an effective deterrent remains to be seen. Again, reading about one rape case does not mean it happens all the time.

Don't flaunt your jewellery no matter how tempted you are to display designer labels.

Don't follow anyone who accosts you with the promise of a real 'bargain price' leather jacket just around the corner in his car! It could be fatal for he could be a mugger. Nine times out of 10, this sort of conman is simply selling stolen goods. Even so, you run the risk of the goods falling apart in no time.

Last but not least, carry some sort of makeshift weapon like a rolled-up umbrella or a spray. At least you can ward off attack if you're big enough. Otherwise pray that it's only your money he wants. Unless you provoke a fight, you are unlikely to be involved in physical violence of any kind. Of course it happens but only you can help prevent the odds of it happening to a great degree.

Out in the country crime rate drops sharply because of your mobility and there are few pockets of urban crowding that breed crime. Still you read about women drivers who, because of a car fault, stop at a motorway point only to be assaulted by some chancer. The police warning is that, should your car develop problems, do not walk away further than you need to. All motorways have emergency phones dotted at convenient distances throughout Britain. If this is not possible, either flag down passing motorists or wait till daylight or the police arrive, if the problem crops up at night.

The Best Insurance

The first thing you do in Britain is to insure yourself properly. Everything from your entire household down to your winter coat. Insurance premiums are low in this country where it is huge business and paying around £30 a month to cover all your worldly belongings makes for easy sleep.

Most banks and building societies will give you complete advice on what is the best package and what coverage you need. For a low monthly outlay you know that, if your roof caves in or an expensive antique is stolen, insurance will cover the cash value, if not the sentimental. This latter can only be protected by adequate burglar alarms which every home should have. It can range from heat-sensing lights that come on when a human comes within a certain distance to those that will wake up the dead should a trespasser trip it. Whatever system you need, there are any number of security systems firms listed in your local directory or the *Yellow Pages*.

FASHION

Fashion pundits of the European market sharpen their needles in the constant battle for trend-setting supremacy; the clamorous claims of Milan, Paris or London being THE sartorial capital hyped up by such glossies as *Vogue*, *Cosmopolitan* and the various rag mags. Despite the likes of such stellar designers as Christian Lacroix – French to the tips of his well-manicured fingernails – and *enfant terrible* Jean Paul Gaultier who gave chic to punk street fashions, English designers defend to the death the far-reaching influences of THEIR designs.

An inadequate overview perhaps, but London – as the undisputed fashion capital, at least of Great Britain – does gobsmack one within a few minutes of strolling down Oxford Street and any suburban high street as multiple chain stores and their smaller cousins stock the very latest, be it outrageous neon-glow pedal pushers or drop dead chic.

Given justifiable human vanity – the British male of the species having more or less shaken off their staid pinstriped suit and conservative image – the stores and boutiques create somewhat conspicuous spending and a constant dilemma.

It takes the most dyed-in-the-wool not to be affected by such elegant offerings, the other dilemma being to spend £25 for chain store jeans or its upmarket designer relative for 10 times as much. I found the most refreshing aspect of dress-codes being a liberal attitude of what is or is not suitable work-wear.

Apart from such serious professions as banking, law and high-finance where the sombre suit (the bowler and furled-up umbrella being rather exclusive to an antiquated attitude), the British pretty much dress as they please.

It can be difficult to tell whether a be-jeaned, pony-tailed hunk is an artistic director or businessman as he is likely to be either! Jeans are not a reflection of sloppiness nor a single earring dangling on a male ear-lobe a glinting hint of decadence. Freedom of expression, in its widest interpretation, is a fundamental right. Unless of course your employer lays down his particular guidelines.

Britain does open the closet doors wide for people who have lived and worked in more restrictive societies where even trousers on women are frowned upon as being too bold.

Peculiarly and even paradoxically, certain clubs still cling to this rule much to the angst of British women who shout very loudly about sexism. A few hallowed bastions of exclusive male clubs have given way to women membership with resigned sighs.

Living in a country where daily wear is highly dependent on the vagaries of weather can present a few problems. You can make some awful (and expensive) mistakes in your early months here but will soon learn how to buy shrewdly. Unless you opt to take yourself out of the fashion rat race altogether, putting together a wardrobe to do battle with biting winter winds, stifling summer heat in the underground or unpredictable wet/dry changes can be fun.

What is comforting is that chain stores are up to the minute with seasonal wear at affordable prices. After this, it's all a matter of keeping a close ear and eye to daily weather reports.

I used to muffle a chuckle seeing someone swamped in a Chaplinesque great coat several sizes too large. The person inside it had the last laugh when a sudden chilling blast hit me in my ribs covered only by a short, cheap bomber jacket purchased more for its style than function. As for those who persist in refusing to invest in a winter coat – three borrowed cardigans only single you out as a visitor and therefore clumsy fodder for snatch thieves – they aren't half as effective as a second-hand duffle coat.

There are any number of second-hand shops usually run by charitable organisations such as Oxfam, which has hundreds of outlets throughout Britain, and street stallholders.

The temptation – especially if you have spare cash – is to go mad and buy a new coat every year. It will soon dawn on a visitor that most chain stores sell the basic garment year in year out with but the subtlest changes in design features. All this is consumer seduction that costs you in terms of outlay and wardrobe space.

Winter garments used about four months of the year take up a lot of space of which there is a premium in most English homes. The weather being what it is, you really need two sets of clothes – spring/summer and autumn/winter wear.

Of course the store and catalogue companies (this is big business) will hit you with new goods every season and resistance can go weak in the face of glitzed-up brochures via the junk mail circuit.

As a practical guideline, if you are staying over a year, your wardrobe must have the following, whether designer label or budget:

• Winter coat, either in wool or fully-lined with water and wind-resistant fabric. This is one item you should not stinge on if it's going to see you through several years. The latter is more practical as it doubles as rain and cold wear.

• A light spring/summer short coat with plenty of pockets. Not only

are they useful for keeping chequebooks, wallets and passports, they are warm duffles for your hands when there is a sudden chill.
- A woollen scarf for those parts of the anatomy garments cannot cover, such as your neck, chin and ears. Winter cold can really hurt those exposed bits.
- A pair of fitting gloves that do not rob your fingers of feeling when you're rummaging for your tube pass or small change. Leather is a good buy as it lasts for ages.
- Comfortable jeans and woollen trousers for the two seasons.
- Good walking shoes and thick socks because cold gets to your feet first.

Outside (or rather inside) these basics, it matters little what you wear next to your skin as there are but a few months in Britain that you can walk about in open-necked shirt and open-toed sandals.

Every decade since the post-war years has seen fashion trends taking root across the nation that in turn influenced what you could buy, even if some were so impractical you could not wear. The 60s perhaps made the most imprint with psychedelic bell-bottoms, mini-skirts, winkle-pickers (pointy-toed, high-heeled shoes for men), back-combed hair and fringed jackets just to name a few. If you are into retro at all and were not around during that period, you'd probably know the 'look' immortalised by Twiggy, Mary Quant and popsters Janis Joplin, The Beatles and films of the genre. Their influence was global and who did not have a pair of bells that picked up more dirt than they were worth?

Thirty years on, fashion is pretty much an important priority among most of us though there is a marked absence of that 'total, pulled-together' look. One finds one's own style amid the welter of clothes churned out by the industry with much wider-ranging styles. Since the 70s, the emphasis has been on individuality rather than prescribed fashion dictates.

In short, you rummage among department stores, street stalls and the inner recesses of your wardrobe for your threads. Cast a

You can wear almost anything in the streets and no one will give you a second glance. Individuality and freedom of expression are the guidelines.

beady eye on street fashions and the rest depends on your individual panache or whatever you deem suitable for work or play.

The very term 'street fashions' is no mere description *per se*. In Britain, it dictates the industry to a degree that unwise indifference to it can be disastrous. As a first-time observer, this mode à la public is captivating and bewildering.

Are spiky green hair, hob-nailed boots and torn jeans a must for parties? Or are cycling shorts in luminous purple what you wear for a summer picnic? Up the market, do you need a designer dress for an executive meeting or a double-breasted Italian suit to impress your interviewer? They all can be termed 'street fashion' in as much as they are what you see in great profusion on the thousands of people scurrying to work, catching buses, cycling or simply clack-clacking down the high street in no particular hurry.

Judge not the strange looking chap in leather trousers, ripped T-shirt and half a ton of jewellery as a symbol of indolent youth. He might very well be an off-duty civil servant simply indulging in his own sartorial fantasy away from office constraints of neat shirt, trousers and tie. By the same token, a woman wearing something that appears to be a gypsy's cast-off could be a high-powered executive on her way to a nightclub.

In the service industry (hotels and department stores in the main) all staff, if not in uniform, are sharply togged out in suits or dresses. Manager or minion, designation and name tagged, package themselves thus. And they travel by public transport.

As a final analysis, people should not be judged on what they wear because it can be highly erroneous and even offensive. In a sense, fashion forges egalitarianism in Britain because every individual enjoys the freedom to dress as he or she pleases, outside whatever parameters that preclude total freedom set by employers.

By the Buy

Chain stores and their several sales a year are a comfort. Sales in

Britain are, praise be, not the token 10% off affair, and if you have a keen eye, you can pick up great buys like a carpet for a fraction of its normal cost.

Sales at clothing stores are particularly chaotic, though, and you should be prepared to jostle and snatch at what you're after with all the elbow power you have. People have been known to queue up in the wee hours of the morning just to pick up a winter coat slashed from £100 to £20. Alas, such bargains are usually one-offs with a thousand other people casting the same beady eye for that garment.

There is no time for dithering as Britain is awash with professional bargain hunters highly skilled at swooping down and hanging on to a cut-price item even as you are diffidently fingering it. At sales time, queues at check-out counters can last forever and there are many pitfalls to look out for.

Many items are less than perfect and trading practices disallow any exchange for sale goods, so beware of factory faults like odd sleeves and torn linings that, given the cost of labour in Britain, can sometimes set you back more than what you have paid for a new garment in the first place.

The key factor really is what you can afford and whether you need a particular item. And don't think that street stalls and factory outlets offer you cut-prices at no expense to quality. The rag trade is a dog-eat-dog world where saving thread in one garment times several thousand units makes the difference in retail pricing. And profit. As such, it is not a 'sale' but more a con.

Department store sales are generally above board and are used to get rid of end-of-season lines. Throw-away chic, as the term goes, dictates sales and prices are slashed simply because a large percentage of the mass buying simply would not buy something considered passé. Never mind that the same people swoop down on the same things when the prices are trimmed drastically. If 'FREE' is the most powerful word in advertising, 'CUT PRICE SALE' comes a close second in consumer seduction.

In the past decade, business people with a sharp sense of consumer habits have made fortunes by producing masses of all kinds of clothing and other accessories, thereby reducing unit prices and putting hitherto expensive things within reach of the budget conscious. A case in point is a nation-wide jewellery chain store that got rid of intimidating shop ambience (it was after all gold and precious stones that they were selling), created bright shop windows without glitz and brought prices down to the masses. In short, the whizz kid businessman got into the head of the consumer and came up with a money-making solution that his predecessors thought beneath them.

Trays of gold jewellery, watches and accessories are displayed without the least pretention and people walk in knowing exactly how much they can spend. Also, they are not greeted by the frosty tones of a toffee-nosed jeweller used only to clients making appointments before coming in. To cut a long story short, the same chain is now worth millions and buying jewellery has no more awe than shopping for vegetables.

This concept has pretty much set the trend for clothing retailers as well, and suddenly, it is as chic to buy from them as from a bespoke boutique that probably charges much more because of smaller turnover.

The most visible clothing store chains that specialise in middle-of-the-road prices are Next (for youngish and trendy fashions), Burton and Coles (for suits) and Laura Ashley (for women's fashion and fabrics). You cannot miss them as there is an outlet in virtually every city and town of any size throughout the country, with new ones opening all the time. Then there are the department stores with clothing on high key like Marks & Spencer, John Lewis and D.H. Evans. John Lewis has a particularly attractive sales pitch under the umbrella catchphrase of 'never knowingly undersold'. In other words, if you can buy a similar item from any other store in the country for less than the John Lewis price tag, they will give you the difference. No doubt professional shoppers thrive on such delicious offering.

Many stores, Marks & Spencer in particular, will exchange goods with no questions asked within a week, should you be unsatisfied with what you bought. Of course you should show your receipt, and the garment's innumerable tags (anti-theft, washing labels, manufacturer's codes, etc.) should not have been removed.

I have never seen more tags than those on clothes sold in Britain. It gets downright bewildering sometimes to know which ones to snip off and which ones to retain so dry-cleaners know what to do.

As of going to print, middle-of-the-road (for basic wear from chain stores) prices mean £25 (trousers), £8 (shirt), £30 (dress), £45 (suit), £80 (winter coat) and £25 (leather shoes). This is a rough guideline as there are too many variables, like where you shop, type of fabric, etc. Rather more 'high class' than high street to use a somewhat antiquated term, are names such as Jaeger (brand as well as store name), Aquascutum, Burberry (their raincoats are practically collector's items) and The Scotch House. They all represent top quality whatever their country of origin or manufacture, even if made in Hong Kong, and prices can be mind boggling.

A Burberry raincoat with signature checked lining and immaculate finish can set you back £400 or more. The option of a similar-looking one with similar (not on close scrutiny) finish in a department store can cost £50 if you are not into the designer tag.

Personally, it makes no sense to pay a lot of money for designer this or that when 10 million people can be seen sporting the same thing! Throw in the Made in Thailand fakes and you've got a real quandary. Still, you've got the snob who refuses to buy anything unless it has someone's name on it or better yet, it comes from a specific store in Knightsbridge.

Harrods is not just a London store, even though it is owned by Arabs and supplied by the same wholesalers to other chain stores. It's a whole image, brimful of undisputed quality or so it seems. I know they sell tat as well but, as a friend says, "at least it's Harrods tat." You can't argue with this kind of loyalty.

Even their shopping bags in green plastic are a status symbol. If it so pleases you to fork out £25 for a scarf with the Harrods label deftly displayed to full advantage, then enjoy. A high street store one lasts just as long, keeps you just as warm for perhaps less than half the price.

Getting the lowdown from my rag trade friends, I discovered that there is still a bias against the 'Made in Hong Kong, Japan, Manila or Singapore' tag. Never mind that cost of labour in Britain has driven just about every manufacturer to seek stitching skills from the East.

Although it is required by law to state the country of manufacture, the tag is usually so well hidden that it gets missed among the half dozen or so others. The other ploy is to place the 'Designed in...' tag prominently. If it is a country like Italy or France, chances are the country of manufacture will matter less.

Several leading British designers have actually set up factories in India, especially for intricate bead and sequin work which Indian craftsmen and women are famous for. And the price tag can be equivalent to a year's wages in India!

Whatever your tastes in clothing are, Britain is a treasure trove of fashion finds. Trendy, conservative, way out or plain outrageous, there's something for every taste and pocket. I have never seen people appear more comfortable in clothes that make you feel uncomfortable just looking at them!

If you're on a budget, putting together a wardrobe for the changes in temperature requires forethought and a strong will. Everywhere you turn, you are seduced by magnificent window displays that are an art unto themselves. Fashion window display experts are highly skilled in creating an aura that is irresistible. Of course when you actually go into the shop and see racks of the same items, the glamour wears off a little. But you're already halfway there, enticed into the shops as the displays are meant to do. But ultimately, common sense must prevail if you don't want to end up owning something that will not see the light of day because you haven't the nerve to wear it. One thing I learnt after eight years: to rid myself of self-consciousness about wearing something a little unconventional. It's great for self-confidence because nobody gives a hoot.

Street Cred

Britain has earned the reputation of being the world's trendsetter for fashion in the broadest sense. British inventiveness is matchless – even if marketing falls short of American go-getting. Nowhere is originality, ingenuity and all the other -ities you can think of more visible than on the streets in London and only slightly more muted in other cities and towns. The ancient, the quaint, eccentric and plain outrageous all co-exist in wonderful pastiche. Individual right is the sacred cow and cries of repression will explode if one so much as decrees a no-no, be it in dress code or architecture. Only in the area of historical heritage will people close ranks and oust the kitsch and contemporary misfits.

Given the variety of styles hobnobbing on the streets, a first-time visitor is apt to get eyeball fatigue. In a packed train, orange hair, nose studs and black-streaked cheeks cause no more than a cursory glance. As much the British penchant for politeness and minding their own business as the fact that it is not deemed decadent. Outlandish maybe. My neighbour used to spend hours putting warpaint on her daughter's face and waxing her hair till it stood up like a foot-high pyramid just so that she could attend a party. It was a startling introduction to a different culture and set of values.

Causes, religious sects and other British eccentricities use the streets to draw attention to their public displays and, hopefully, win more people over to their side.

Pop Culture

Whatever the current pop culture, British streets provide the most colourful backdrop for the inevitable spillover. Ever since the 50s,

Britain has exerted the most powerful influence in trendsetting, each new cult – usually riding on the backs of teenagers – being greeted with consternation by parents, great glee by the popular press and a little alarm by the authorities.

From the Teddy Boy era with their drain pipe trousers and natty jackets to the androgynous likes of David Bowie and Boy George, street cred – short for credibility – has always reflected the mode and behaviour of these role models. And they strut in their threads as if on mobile parade reflecting the same merchandise in store windows.

In the heyday of Boy George, the most outrageous gender-bender the pop world has known, British youth went to town with this new freedom of sexual fusion. Boy George is a strapping six-footer who wears full make-up, ribbons, bells and it seems everything he could lay his hands on from his sister's cosmetics kit. He spawned a cult following not only with his music but his penchant for cross-dressing. Among the many youths who took to this flamboyance were Orientals, Japanese mainly.

Over the past three decades, the pop bandwagon has taken on and unloaded the lot – drugs, fashion, promiscuity, a spectrum of music from the sublime to the ridiculous – but its manifestation on British streets today is less cohesive. What with the constant need for revivalism, 60s strut exists in tandem with 80s yuppiesm.

Where music was the unifying force behind the somewhat loose ideology of the hippy 60s, of flower power, the Beatles, mini-skirts, bell bottoms and Eastern religions, it has been largely taken over by slick media and commercial packaging. There was, even if briefly, a specific 'yuppie look' of short-cropped hair, flannel blazers, filofaxes and other newly-rich trappings. Even clothing stores had merchandise devoted to this look.

In the aftermath of the hyped-up Batman movie, Britain virtually exploded with bat-mania. Store windows, babies, old age pensioners, hoardings, radio, TV and pedestrians sported one or the other caped crusader's costume. Where else could one show off such zapp and kapow except in the streets?

DIRT

Nothing comes more as an initial shock when arriving in a country than its state of public cleanliness – or rather uncleanliness. Britain suffers the ignominy of being one of the dirtiest nations in the world. This grimy state of affairs has had the former prime minister, Mrs Margaret Thatcher, actually picking up sweet wrappings and drink cans in the hope of setting an example. Whether this gesture has moved the millions of Britain's litterbugs is yet to be seen.

Just what has made the country, a few decades ago a rustic elegy of pastoral greenness surrounding urban tidiness, so filthy? The finger of blame is firmly pointed in the direction of the takeaway purveyors, usually of food. Containers by the millions are simply chucked indiscriminately on the streets, on trains and buses and from them.

Vandals and graffiti artists add the blighted backdrop to this heap of greasy fast food jetsam. Residents blame visitors and civic-minded visitors blame those who have no such inclination. But accusations come to nought because little action has been taken until now, when the debris from years of littering has reached epic proportions.

Parliament is now preparing to pass a Green Bill that will give ordinary citizens the power to take councils and public bodies to court for despoiling public areas. Anti-litter laws have been around for a long time but are hardly ever implemented. The law is usually too busy with more urgent matters like sniffing out drug merchants and hunting real criminals. Now councils intend to impose a minimum fine of £10 on litter louts, and serious offences might have a hefty tag of £1000.

It isn't just litter because litter begets grime which in turn becomes dust. I have seen Japanese men and women walking around

London wearing curious nostril covers as protection, no doubt, against the polluted air. They, after all, come from a country that sets complete store by cleanliness, both at home and in the street.

It will come as an alarming sight to see, especially in London, people blatantly littering not only streets but public transport and in full view of dozens of other people. Few have the nerve to say anything because the litterbug is often abusive when taken to task. Some even become violent. As a rule, if you see an individual hurling a beer can across a tube carriage, let an alarm bell ring in your head that he could be deliberately calling attention to his bravado. It could be dangerous to confront him, however diplomatic you may be. It is a different matter if an organisation falls foul of litter laws. You can report this to the proper authority.

London is by no means the dirtiest city in Britain (though part of one of the dirtiest boroughs!) if the most visible and maligned though it is largely the fault of daily commuters, visitors and the sheer volume of the takeaway trade. Other places have been identified and tarnished with the same brush. The Department of the Environment, alarmed as they are at the outcry of the brutalising effect such an environment would have on society, can only do so much.

Much more really depends on the individual and how he responds to the inculcation of civic-mindedness. Thousands of visitors and migrants to Britain come from countries where public hygiene is either feeble or non-existent. Throwing away a can onto the street is simply an echo of a rural habit.

Garbage collection also plays a part in the accumulation of Britain's filth. In most city centres, this is done everyday, sometimes several times a day. In the suburbs, it is more often than not weekly. In theory that is. I have been through as long as three weeks where my garbage remained uncollected and building up putrifying matter and smell. Scavenger dogs and cats complete the job by spreading it around the neighbourhood, but not before leaving the bulk at my front door.

You simply live with the knowledge that in any given month, your garbage may not be collected more than twice. Even the regulation black garbage bags given to most households by their respective boroughs cannot provide enough insulation against rotting food. As for the city centres, even multiple daily collections cannot keep up with the volume, and uncollected rubbish usually ends up as dogs' dinners spread across pedestrian malls and streets.

In windy weather, litter bags and unwrapped rubbish go their own merry ways fouling up even more than a pack of scavenger dogs can do. Restaurants are the biggest culprits here as their swill can amount to a small lorry load every evening. Even tied up in bags, swill can ferment remarkably fast in summer.

Takeaway joints have no jurisdiction over what their customers do with their empty burger boxes but they have given them the ammunition to add to this junk food. Perhaps 'junk food' is an apt name because the junk refers not only to what you put in your stomach but also to what is thrown away.

CULTURAL QUIZ

QUIZ 1

You have been working in the London office of your company for some time now. It is Friday evening and your colleagues are about to 'hit' the pubs before heading home, as they have been doing all the time you've been here. Having settled in more, you've now become 'one of the lads' and they have asked you to join them. You are generally teetotal and have a long way to travel home. Your reaction is:

A Demur politely saying that you don't drink and want to get home as soon as possible.

B React with annoyance when they persist and firmly refuse, even lecturing them for drinking too much, having heard many 'Monday morning after' stories about their various stages of inebriation on such nights out.

C Rationalise with them that even an hour after office closing will see rush hour traffic, so what's the point?

D Show enthusiasm, commenting that you will go along but will only have a small drink if it's alright with them.

Comment

This Friday-evening ritual is fairly common especially among unmarried people who see no reason to rush home from work. It is as much a social thing as practical evasive action for rush hour traffic, and the 'matey' feeling over a few drinks is important among most British workers. It is an opportunity to generally let their hair down away from the constraints of office rules. Even get a little drunk as a reward for a hard week's work. They will not belittle you about being teetotal though a few will show surprise that you don't even drink beer which is a national brew practically. Option D will not only give you the opportunity to get to know them but also give an insight into a typical slice of British life – the pub scene. Non-drinking aliens are often astonished at how much a Brit gets down in one evening.

QUIZ 2

You have been asked to join a colleague and his friends for a meal after work. It is a sort of casual 'come along with us' invitation and not a 'be my guest' gesture. You have a good meal and when the bill is presented, your friend takes out his wallet to pay, and perhaps to your surprise, his friends do the same. Your reaction is:

A You make no attempt to foot your share, feeling embarassed about this 'Dutch' treat and surprised at your friend's tight fist.

B Feel insulted that you should have to pay as you were invited and cover up by insisting to pay the whole bill. Even throwing in casually that it is not the done thing where you come from.

C Do as the others do without any feeling of discomfiture, commenting casually that it is not the done thing where you come from.

Comment

Unless it is specifically made clear that you are a special guest, or your host is giving a business lunch or dinner, when you are asked to join in a group for a meal, going Dutch is always the norm. It is common practice in Britain where everyone at table shares the cost of a meal at the same time – even down to presenting different credit cards to the waiter. There's nothing to be embarrassed about this, no matter how high-powered your dinner group is. Nor does it reflect that one is tightfisted, simply economics. If it is a formal dinner, but common pool, the practice remains the same. Thus C is your best option.

QUIZ 3

You have just emerged from a railway or tube station and need directions to get to your place of appointment. You have an address but have no idea of the local layout of side streets and house numbering system which can be confusing in British cities. What you do know is that it's quite near to the station. Your reaction is to:

A Ask the nearest tradesman – usually a newsvendor or fruiterer – expecting him or her to know the environs.
B Catch someone you think seems local, i.e. it's not a bag-laden tourist but well-dressed type probably working in the area.
C Ask the first person to pass near you in the station.
D Go to the station ticket/information counter.

Comment

Depending on whether it's a city, town or village you are at, the options vary. Tradesmen outside busy train stations can often be tetchy and unhelpful not because they do not know, but because they get asked constantly. They may know the local landmarks but are likely to profess no knowledge of a specific road, street or building. The 'local' looking person may very well be in the same boat as you, especially in a big city where most workers are familiar only with the patch around their place of work. Whoever you ask, do not be offended if the person is dismissive. Your best bet is the station information counter. The cardinal rule is to be clear about your query and, when someone says he doesn't know, do not badger him or seem to doubt him.

QUIZ 4

You are sitting on a bench in a park and someone (British) sits down next to you. He gives you a brief nod and a half-smile but makes no attempt to say anything. It is a nice day and you feel chatty. You attempt to make conversation, but get monosyllabic answers. Your reaction is:

A Continue making conversation even if the other person simply smiles and does not respond beyond cryptic replies.

B Leave off and leave the person alone but maintain friendly 'body language'. It's hard to define this but if someone sitting next to you throws out unfriendly vibes, a sidelong glance, a look in the eye – for whatever reason – you'd soon feel the insidious un-friendliness.

C Get huffy and leave, convinced that the British reputation for being cold and aloof is well-earned.

Comment

While it is generally true that the British are reserved, most respond to casual, impersonal conversation especially in an informal setting like a park or a railway station. There is a difference between 'reserved' and 'aloof'. Do not persist if the person does not wish to talk or throws out vibes telling you so; he may simply be a private person not given to instant rapport with a stranger. When you get a smile and a nod it still does not mean the person wishes to talk. Stick to the weather if you feel really voluble. It will garner a few comments anyway or even break the ice. It is rare that you will hit off a close friendship with a Brit within a few hours.

QUIZ 5

You are in an exclusive knitwear section of a department store where goods are not on general display but folded up, out of touch. You are in a great hurry and need to buy a present, specifically a sweater in a certain size. You are not sure of the design but eye a range within your budget. You would like a closer look and feel.

Every salesperson seems to be engaged. Your reaction is:

A Barge in while a salesperson is dealing with another customer and expect to be served. Show annoyance when told to wait.

B Wait patiently until you spy a free salesperson.

C Look around for the item yourself, reach out to a shelf and pull it down. It is what you are looking for and march to the checkout counter.

D Leave the store in disgust after waiting what seems like eternity for service.

Comment

Most British stores – even small shops – have cut-to-the-bone staff and, unless trade is slow, you will rarely find staff approaching you. No matter how long-winded another customer is engaging a salesperson, you simply have to wait. None will ask to be of service while dealing with another person. The first rule is to look for the merchandise yourself and seek help only if you must, like in this situation. Otherwise, it is cash-and-carry. Do not simply pull things off shelves. There is simply no hurrying a salesperson or checkout cashier if a transaction is going on. Never jump a queue. Don't shop in a rush.

QUIZ 6

Your car is involved in a minor accident with another vehicle but with no serious damage. You both get out amid heavy traffic to sort it out. Your reaction is:

A Extreme annoyance – if the other driver is at fault – and you begin to berate the person while traffic is building up around you.

B Get out of the car and without rancour, ask for relevant details like insurance policy number, licence number, etc., and go on your way quickly.

C Come to an amiable agreement without taking down details and leave.

Comment

It is always prudent to take down details and report the accident no matter how minor, unless there is no visible damage. Making a public scene is not done and will only raise hackles unnecessarily. If you are not at fault, there is still no reason to rankle as insurance will cover for all damages. It is bad form to conduct a shouting match in the middle of a busy road. Just as it is to toot your horn when caught in a traffic jam which neither you nor the other drivers involved can do anything about. Generally, British drivers are very sanguine and polite – whether involved in accidents or caught in a snarl up.

ADDRESSES AND
RECOMMENDED READING

USEFUL ADDRESSES
Arts Council of Britain
105 Piccadilly
London W1
Tel: 071 333 0100

Association of Commonwealth Universities
36 Gordon Square
London W1
Tel: 071 387 8572

Australian High Commission
Australia House
The Strand
London WC1
Tel: 071 438 8000

Automobile Association
24-hr breakdown service and general/home touring information
Station Road, Cheadle
Cheshire SK8 7BS
Tel: 061 458 6000

British Council Headquarters
10 Spring Gardens
London SW1
Tel: 071 930 8466

The British Library Board and Press Office
2 Sheraton Street
London W1
Tel: 071 636 1544

British Nursing Association
443 Oxford Street
London W1
Tel: 071 629 9030

British Tourist Authority
Thames Tower
Black Road
Hammersmith
London W6 9 EC
Tel: 081 846 9000

Electricity Board Head Office
81 High Holborn
London WC1
Tel: 071 242 9050

Department of Social Security
Headquarters Office
Richmond House
79, Whitehall
London SW 1A 2NS
Tel: 071 210 5983

British Gas Corporation
152 Grosvenor Road
London SW1
Tel: 071 821 1444

British Home Office (Immigration Department)
Wellesley Road
Croydon
Tel: 081 686 0688

The Buddhist Society
58, Eccleston Square
London SW1
Tel: 071 834 5858

Hindu Centre
39, Grafton Terrace
London NW5
Tel: 081 458 8200

Malaysia, Office of the High Commissioner
45, Belgrave Square
London SW1
Tel: 071 235 8033

Mosque and Islamic Centre of Brent
Chichele Road
London NW2
Tel: 081 452 7403

Singapore High Commission
Chancery, 2 Wilton Terrace
London SW1
Tel: 071 235 8315

Students and Consular Dept
5, Chesham Street
London SW1
Tel: 071 235 9067

The Royal Thai Embassy
30, Queen's Gate
London SW7
Tel: 071 589 0173

RECOMMENDED READING

There are more books about Britain than a whole library can contain and the list here must be seen in the light of scratching the surface of published information. Even so, each provides much in-depth information in the areas of history, travel, social norms, entertainment and food.

General

The Customs and Ceremonies of Britain. An encyclopaedia of living traditions. Thames and Hudson.
Great Britain, An Insight Guide. Apa Productions.
Britain Discovered. A pictorial atlas of the land and the heritage; consultant for the book: Arthur Marwick. Artists House.
250 Tours of Britain. Drive Publications Ltd for the Automobile Association.
Images of Britain. A tribute to Britain's rich heritage. The Automobile Association.
The Times Museum and Galleries Passport Guide 1990. Spero Communications.
Explore Britain – 1001 Places to Visit. George Philip & Son.

Food
The Complete Farmhouse Kitchen Cookbook. Collins in association with Yorkshire Television. Many traditional British recipes.
English Seafood Cookery. An A-Z of fish cookery. Richard Stein.

DIY
Collins Complete DIY Manual. A veritable self-help bible of hints, instructions and step-by-step guides to do everything yourself – from plumbing to double-glazing.

Maps
Philips Road Atlas of Britain 1991. With 80 city plans, local radio stations and tourist information.
The RAC Motoring Atlas of Britain.

Educational
The Parents' Guide to Independent Schools. SFIA Educational Trust, SFIA House, 15 Forlease Road, Maidenhead, Berkshire SL6 1JA.
Which School? Gabbitas Truman & Thring, 6/8 Sackville Street, London W1X 2BR.
The Schools of the United Kingdom. Ed. J. Burrow & Co. Ltd, Publicity House, Streatham Hill, London SW2 4TR.

Additional Bibliography
The Making of Modern English Society from 1850. Janet Roebuck, Routledge & Kegan Paul.
Friends in High Places – Who Runs Britain. Jeremy Paxman, Penguin, 1990.
Everybody's Historic England – A History and Guide. Jonathan Kiek, Quiller Press.
John Bull's Island – Immigration and British Society 1871-1971. Colin Holmes, Macmillan.

Change in British Society. A.H. Halsey, Oxford University Press.
The Age of Parody. Ascerbic observations on contemporary British manners and styles. Philip Norman, Hamish Hamilton.
The Politics of Race and Residence. Susan Smith, Polity Press.
The Country Year. A nature watcher's calendar and field guide. Geoffrey Young, George Philip.
Geoffrey Grigson's Countryside. The classic companion to rural Britain. Ebury Press.
We British – Britain under the Microscope. Eric Jacobs and Robert Worcester, Weidenfield & Nicholson.
Rail Atlas of Great Britain and Ireland. The only publication detailing the present-day network in its entirety. Oxford Publishing Company.
Britain 1990. An Official Yearbook. Her Majesty's Stationery Office.
An A-Z of British Life. Adrian Room, Oxford University Press.

THE AUTHOR

Born in Singapore, Terry Tan first trained as a broadcaster and worked as a radio producer for 10 years. He also did some television presenting for news and other entertainment programmes. He later switched to advertising as a copy writer and then as a features/food writer for the now defunct *Sunday Nation*. His first cookbook was published in 1979 and he has written seven to date. In 1983, Terry moved to England as a restaurant consultant and he is currently a freelance culinary writer for several British magazines and other publishing groups, writing on food and other topical subjects. Terry is also well-known on television, having broadcast over the BBC on several occasions, and taping a cooking programme for Satellite Television and a pilot for the BBC general interest programme *Bazaar*.

INDEX